The Dumb Gringo

How Not to Be One in Missions

By Fred C. Collom

PRESS

Contents

Preface vii

Chapter 1: Compelling Factors and the Book of Acts..............9

Chapter 2: Hudson Taylor Revisited......................................31

Chapter 3: A New Kid on the Block: The New Breed 49

Chapter 4: Colonial Missionary Complex 71

Chapter 5: The Dumb Gringo: Funny Dumb, Little Dumb,
Pretty Dumb, and Big Dumb 89

Chapter 6: Money and Missions...107

Chapter 7: The Mazatlán Four-Point Strategy.......................125

To Sum It Up...145

Why Another Book on Missions?

Over the years, I have witnessed people doing "stupid" things in missions, despite having read the popular books on the subject. This book is not a profound theological work, but it does deal with practical issues such as money, conduct, and attitude. I have seen intelligent people who have read all the books on missions behaving as "Dumb Gringos," without realizing the damage they were doing.

The author began his ministry in Central Mexico where he pioneered several churches in towns where no evangelical church had been successfully planted before. At times, the opposition to his ministry included death threats. In 1981, he, his wife and three-month-old daughter were hit head-on by a drunk driver. They were all severely injured and were air lifted out of Mexico in serious condition. Rumors spread that his short missions career was over. However, a few months later, they returned to Mexico.

In his twenty-five years of experience working in Mexico, he has been involved in planting eighteen churches. He has also established nine children's feeding centers, started four medical/dental clinics, and set up a school for the children of the "dump scroungers." His ministry operates mobile clinics and mobile kitchens that minister to the poor. He has also developed a program that helps short-term missions groups be successful in their endeavors.

CHAPTER 1

Compelling Factors and the Book of Acts

Many people think the Book of Acts is a manual for how to do modern missions. Other groups and churches use it as a source for forming their church doctrine. I think both courses of action are unwise unless you take into account what I call "Compelling Factors." Compelling Factors were those things present in the culture in the first-century world that influenced the way missions operated and the decisions that were made in regard to them.

I want to mention that I don't know if someone before me has used the term *Compelling Factors* or not. If so, then give them the credit. If not, you can pin it on me.

Examples of churches forming doctrines from the Book of Acts are the United Pentecostals or Apostolic Pentecostals, and others known as "Jesus only." They base salvation on Acts 2:38 where Peter commended the hearers to be baptized in the name of Jesus. The early church baptized in the name of Jesus, so that is the way the true church must do it. This leads to other errors. Because they believe in the inspiration of the Scriptures, they have to reconcile Mathew 28:19–20 where Jesus said to baptize in the name of the Father, Son, and Holy Spirit. They reason that, since it says "the name of " (singular) and not "the names of" (plural), the Father, the

Son, and the Holy Spirit, Peter must have had a revelation that Jesus is the name of the Father and Holy Spirit. Their Book of Acts doctrine also leads many to believe that you are not saved until you speak in tongues. Some go so far as to teach that even if you speak in tongues but are baptized in the name of the Father, Son, and the Holy Spirit, you are not saved. You must be baptized in the name of Jesus only.

An experience that I had with a group years ago taught me to be aware of potential problems in relying too heavily on the Book of Acts for doctrine and practices. I had come into contact with a group called "Christ Tent Ministry" (not its real name), which was headquartered in Illinois and later moved to El Paso, Texas. Members were a product of the Jesus movement and started a traveling tent ministry. They had a passion for missions and began to send teams to other countries. From the outside they looked like a solid group, but as we got to know them, we became aware of a major flaw. They taught that to be a really committed Christian, you had to sell everything and have all things in common like the early church. They believed that was the true church model. To join them, you were exhorted to sell everything and give your money to them for the good of the whole group. At first, we didn't think it was that much of a problem because of all the positive things they were doing. I did have several friends that joined them for a time and then left the group despite the strong exhortation that they were going back to the world after putting their hand to the plow.

However, I didn't realize that their doctrine could produce deadly results until I had a personal experience with them. I was living in Mexico in the city of Fresnillo. To the north was Rio Grande, with a population of around 60,000. I wanted to hold a tent crusade there but didn't have a tent big enough for what I wanted to do, so I invited "Christ Tent Ministry" to come with a team and their tent. A young man named Chris was with the team. He was a blue-eyed, blond, baby-faced kid, with a very good disposition. The Mexicans took to him and the girls adored him. Chris was also a diabetic, which I didn't know at the time. Chris became either discouraged or homesick and wanted to leave the ministry and go home. The problem was he didn't have any money. All of the members depended on the team to meet their needs. He asked the team leader for bus money and was refused. The leader had bought into the doctrine that to leave the ministry was to look back after putting your hand to the plow. I didn't know that this was going on until it was too late.

Chris was upset and went with one of our pastors to the town of Calera, which was approximately seventy-five miles away. He forgot to take his insulin with him and began feeling sick. By the time they got the insulin to him, he was already very ill. They then realized that they needed to get him to a hospital at the border. Jim, who was the same team leader who had refused Chris bus money, packed up his bus camper and headed to El Paso, Texas. Jim didn't fill up with gas before he left, got down the road, and then found that no stations were open. I have often wondered how someone could be so stupid. He had to park at a gas station and wait for it to open the next morning. By then it was too late. Chris was gravely ill. The next morning, Jim made his way to the city of Torreon and hospitalized Chris, who died the next day. This ministry's Book of Acts doctrine had restrained them from doing the right thing in giving Chris the bus money to go home. I never even knew Chris's last name, and I have often wondered what the group told his parents.

I have used a couple of obvious examples to establish the fact that it is possible to improperly establish a doctrine or do missions based on the Book of Acts. What were the compelling factors that "Christ Tent Ministry" missed? With all of their zeal and the anti-establishment influence from the hippie movement, they didn't analyze the Scriptures very well.

Several factors need to be taken into account to understand why the Jerusalem church sold all their goods and had all things common. First, in New Testament times, there was a group of people, many of whom had personally seen the Resurrected Christ and experienced Pentecost, who believed that the Kingdom of God was soon to be set up. To compound matters, a false doctrine had circulated among the brethren that Jesus would return before John would die. This is recorded in the Gospel of John, chapter 20, when Jesus responded to Peter's question about John after Jesus prophesied to Peter how he would die. Peter then asked, "What about him?"

referring to John. Jesus answered in so many words that it was none of Peter's business, when He said, "If I will that he should tarry until I come, what's it to you." This saying spread like wildfire, and I think that it played a role in the Jerusalem church selling all of their goods. They thought Jesus was returning that soon. It became a compelling factor and, in this case, an erroneous one. Many years later when the Gospel of John was written, the author explained that Jesus had never said that John wouldn't die before his return but that he only had stated, "If I will that he tarry." The compelling factors that influenced the church to sell all and practice communal life were a heightened zeal as a result of the resurrection, the supernatural visitation on the day of Pentecost, and possibly the spread of the false doctrine that Jesus would return before the death of John.

Another practice that some churches derive from Acts is electing deacons, which is based on Acts chapter 6. Is this the pattern for New Testament churches, or are there compelling factors that influenced this action? I believe that there were two compelling factors. First, the church had grown so fast that they didn't have a personal relationship with very many of the people. Under normal circumstances you get to know people, build a relationship with them, and then choose leaders accordingly. However, because of the explosive growth, this process was short-circuited. They didn't know who was qualified to lead or who had a good testimony, especially among the Hellenistic Jews.

Second, a major problem was brewing because of the fast growth and the existence of two distinct social groups. These groups were the Hebrew Jews and the (Hellenistic) Greek Jews. With the growth of the church, the Apostles (who were all Hebrew Jews) put those in as leaders who were in relationship with them and were also Hebrew Jews. By then a large part of the church was made up of Greek-speaking Jews who were born or raised outside Israel and had become culturally Greek. Many of the Hebrew Jews felt superior to them. That superior attitude may have existed in the church as well. Whether the superior attitude was real or not, the Greek Jews felt that they were being shortchanged when the food was handed out since all those in control were the Hebrew Jews.

With the compelling factors of a church split and not knowing who was the most qualified among the Greeks, the Apostles realized and accepted that there was an imbalance in the leadership, and to avoid a worst-case scenario, they needed a quick response. They acted accordingly, and several Greek Jews were added to the leadership team, avoiding the split.

I remember reading about a church that experienced explosive growth because of the Jesus movement. Within a few months there were hundreds of new converts, and more were added each week. The pastor knew that he had to have many new leaders. Because of all of the compelling factors, those who had been saved for only three months or more were installed as deacons. There were so many new converts that they became "veterans." This actually worked. Would I do it under normal circumstances? No way. Only with compelling factors can it be done and be directed by the Holy Spirit.

Once while traveling, I visited a Baptist church. That night they were baptizing several people, and before each person was baptized, the pastor would ask, "Does anyone here have any objection to him [or her] being baptized?" When there was no negative reply, he continued and baptized the person. I sat there wondering why he was doing that. Sometime later, I was reading in the Book of Acts where Peter went to Cornelius and shared the Gospel, resulting in his conversion. As he prepared to baptize the new converts, he asked, "Can any man forbid water that these should not be baptized?" I realized why the church that I had visited acted as they did: it was because that was how Peter did it in the Book of Acts.

I think that the compelling factor here is obvious. A company of Jews had joined Peter on his trip to Caesarea. Most of them believed that Gentiles had to first be circumcised and keep the law to be saved. They witnessed the conversion of the Gentiles, and to make it quite clear, the Holy Spirit came upon them and they began to speak in tongues. Then Peter, wanting to make sure that they had understood and accepted this, asked the Jews, "Can any man forbid water that these should not be baptized?"

Now that you know what I mean by compelling factors, let's move on to the question "Is the Book of Acts a 'How to Do Missions' book or not?" Over the years, I have seen many curious examples of what would be considered compelling factors from the

Book of Acts that some have used to do missions. Once again, these are obvious examples. What I am trying to establish is that you can adopt methods and strategies from the Book of Acts and not be successful.

Some churches and missions groups use as their main method door-to-door evangelism because Acts 20:20 mentions Paul having taught publicly, as well as house to house. Others preach at the marketplaces or town square because Paul did so at Athens in Acts 17:17.

When I lived in Fresnillo in central Mexico, I met a young Mexican couple who had moved there to plant a church. They rented a small place and painted the name of their church on the building. Every day, the young man would go downtown to the plaza with his megaphone and preach to those gathered there. As we were talking one day, it became clear that he thought it was the way Paul did it. He asked me why I didn't go to the plaza and proclaim the Gospel. The way he asked the question seemed like he was saying, "Why aren't you wimps boldly preaching the Gospel like me?" In less than a year they packed up and left. Their methods, based on their interpretation of the Book of Acts, didn't bear fruit.

Let us move on to some examples that may not be as obvious. In 1995, when I moved from Fresnillo to Mazatlán, a larger city on Mexico's west coast, I was told that the head of missions in the denomination that I am involved in thought that it was a step in the right direction. He saw Mazatlán as a more important city than the smaller city of Fresnillo in central Mexico. In the Book of Acts, Paul went to all of the major cities in the Roman Empire and planted churches. That sounds like a good strategy, so who could argue with that? Is this a biblical mandate by which we should do missions work and church planting? I don't think so. There were many compelling factors at play that made it the only practical strategy to use in the first-century Roman Empire:

- **Factor 1: The infrastructure**—Rome had built roads between all of the main cities for the rapid movement of troops. These same roads would make travel easier for the first-century missionaries.

- **Factor 2: A universal language**—Greek had become the universal trade language. In all of the major cities, many people spoke Greek, and many interpreters were also available.
- **Factor 3: Few established churches**—Not many churches were established yet. The cities were the only sensible place to start, with thousands of inhabitants living in a small area. To start in the countryside would have been foolish. The difficulty of travel in the country, along with the language barrier, made Paul's strategy of starting with the larger cities the only obvious and practical one.
- **Factor 4: The synagogue**—In nearly all of these Roman cities, you could find established Jewish synagogues. Acts 15:21 states, "For Moses from ancient generations has in every city those who preach him, since he is read in the synagogues every Sabbath." They would play a big role in Paul's strategy. They became his pool for finding workers. Making converts who already had knowledge of God and the Scriptures, and who were free from the deceptions of idols, allowed Paul to accelerate his church endeavors. By first evangelizing in the synagogues, Paul made converts who already had a good knowledge of Scripture. These converts had higher moral standards than the Greeks and Romans, and they were able to battle the deceptions of idols. This allowed Paul to accelerate his church planting.
- **Factor 5: The gentile God Fearers**—The gentiles, who had been attracted by the higher morality of the Jewish religion, were also attached to the synagogues. They also had knowledge of God and had rejected idols. This group, known as the God Fearers, did not want to go through the circumcision ritual to become full-fledged Jewish converts, but they wanted to follow God and hear His word. When Paul showed up with the good news that you could be in fellowship with God without someone with a dirty knife cutting you, they really responded.

This group of converts gave him an incredible advantage in his church planting. What a great fishing pool for men and women who had the potential for leadership and for a core group for a new church plant.

These are the positive compelling factors that influenced Paul's missionary strategy. However, they are not mandates that should guide all church-planting movements or mission work. The same compelling factors are not in play today. They are always changing and should be considered whenever you form your mission strategy.

How would Paul do missionary work if he were living today, with the compelling factors of our time? Of course, we can only speculate. However, I am sure that today's factors would influence how the Holy Spirit would lead him. If Paul were here today, he might not use his first-century strategy. He might head straight to the 10/40 window. I am sure he would surprise us all. A missions leader in a contemporary church movement once pointed out how Paul, on his first missionary journey, was able to make converts and establish elders much faster than is happening today. I believe he was saying that modern missionaries should be able to do it just as fast. I think that, once again, compelling factors played a role in Paul's success.

Have you ever wondered whether Paul, if he were here today and went to the same places, would have the same results he did in the first century? To be honest, I don't think he would. Would he be more successful than I am? I don't doubt that he would. However, I don't believe that Paul would be as successful today in the same places because, since the first century, the world has changed, and so have the positive compelling factors. Besides the positive compelling factors that I have mentioned, there were other factors in play that made it possible to plant a church and leave it in a shorter time. Please note that I am not making an excuse for mission groups' and missionaries' inability to plant churches and raise up indigenous leadership in a reasonable amount of time. What I am saying is that you can't study Paul and make his time frame for church planting a universal law for all countries. Each country will have its positive and negative compelling factors.

What are some of the other factors that I think were present that helped Paul establish churches? One key factor was that there was no dominant universal religion. Another factor was that the Christianity that Paul brought was clearly distinct from the regional religions in the places where he planted churches. The Christians didn't use icons, whereas the pagan temple was full of them. It was easy to grasp and understand the contrasts. In today's world, Islam dominates some of the places where Paul preached. They are already brainwashed into thinking that all non-Muslims are infidels. They have laws forbidding anyone to leave the Muslim religion. They won't allow missionaries to preach about Christ. I think Paul would have a more difficult time making converts today.

Another factor that would be missing is the Jewish synagogue. The large number of gentile God Fearers at the great fishing pool were easy to convert. I am sure Paul would have to develop a whole new strategy if he were here today.

Other factors are in play today that Paul didn't have to deal with. For one thing, in many non-Muslim countries, several branches of Christianity and cults already exist. For example, in Mexico, when we go somewhere to plant a church, very often the Jehovah's Witnesses have already been there. Sometimes the Mormons have been there as well. Can you see the difference? You go to a town to plant a church and the Mormons, Jehovah's Witnesses, Roman Catholics, and possibly others are already there. Some of them can look really Christian. With these groups all claiming to be the only true one and all claiming to believe in Christ, it can make evangelism much more difficult. It can also require more time to establish the elders and release the church.

You may be thinking that if you had signs and wonders like Paul had, you might make more converts. I wish I could say that I have had as many or more signs than Paul had, but I can't. Even so, I have had some dramatic signs with interesting results. When I lived in central Mexico, one night a woman showed up at a cell group. She had been sick for some time and had been to many doctors and specialists without improvement. We prayed for her, and she was instantly healed. Months of constant pain disappeared in a second. She came to church one Sunday and didn't return again, so we went to visit her to see what the problem was. She explained that her son came to her house when he heard that she attended our church. He told her that if she continued to attend, she would no longer have a son. He would disown her. After rebuking her for having left the "true religion," he demanded that she choose him or the Vineyard, stating that if she chose the Vineyard, he would never come and see her again. She chose her son.

Another example of a powerful miracle that bore no fruit in the way of converts also happened in central Mexico. We had a small tent that would hold around 100 people. We would move it around to different neighborhoods and have small evangelistic campaigns. One night we gave an invitation for anyone who had a prayer request to come forward. It seemed like everyone responded. As we were trying to minister to the large number of people requesting prayer, I noticed an elderly woman approaching, and she was carrying a young girl who was about seven or eight years old. I still remember that as she approached, the Holy Spirit showed me that the child had a demon spirit on her. Since there were so many waiting for prayer, I simply rebuked the spirit and continued to minister to others. What I didn't know at the time was that the girl had never walked since birth. The next night, the grandmother returned to the tent carrying the girl. She sat her down and the girl began walking. Everyone was oohing and ahhing, and I didn't know why. We found out about the great miracle that God had performed, and we thought surely the family would respond to the Gospel that we proclaimed every night. This was not so. The parents never came to the tent, and the grandmother never showed up again at church.

The next example happened in Mazatlán. We had a church group visiting us from the United States, and we took them to an area near downtown where they performed some street dramas, followed by the preaching of the Gospel, after which we gave an invitation to anyone who wanted to receive Christ or had a prayer request. One man in his late twenties or early thirties asked for prayer. "What do you want God to do for you?" I asked him. "I'm blind," he explained. He was scheduled for surgery the following week. I prayed for him, and when I finished he just stood there in the street with his eyes closed for the longest time. Suddenly he began to shout, "I can see! I can see!" I was confident he would respond by giving his heart to Christ. He came to church once and didn't return. When we visited him to see why, he informed me that the soccer league had their game the same time that the church service started, and he wanted to play soccer.

One time in central Mexico, I decided to do a little survey to see what the most effective thing that God used to convert those who had become a part of our church in Fresnillo. My assumption was that the dominant factor would be a healing miracle. To my astonishment, the majority replied that the Christian films that we showed was the main thing that God used to cause their conversion. At that time, we had rented a large facility downtown that used to be a farm tractor dealership. It had a warehouse that we used for church meetings and offices. There was a large open area outside where tractors were displayed. We built a large movie screen, and on Sunday nights when it got dark, we would project Christian movies. Usually the movie would start a little before the service ended. It became quite popular. To my surprise, the largest group of converts had been converted by coming to the movies on Sundays. After a while, they would come early and listen at the door of the church. Then they started coming to the service. Talk about a challenge to my kingdom theology. How could this be? Movies were getting more converts than healing miracles! That is the truth of the matter.

What was the compelling factor that caused the movies to become so fruitful? During those days, in the early eighties, there were only two television channels in all of Mexico, and they were government-owned stations. Need I say more? They weren't worth watching. These channels were black and white, while the Vineyard was showing color movies. People began to attend, not necessarily because they were hungry for God but because we had the best show in town. It became the Sunday night ritual for many people. The fact that they heard the Gospel Sunday after Sunday bore fruit, and several converts were made.

Am I saying that healings and miracles aren't important? No, not by any means, but we had discovered something that, for a short time, had more success converting people than the miracles. Soon, that window of opportunity would close. Mexico opened up and

American movies dominated. The Mexican government allowed private companies to start television stations. The compelling factor had changed again, and we were no longer the best show in town.

It is not the same world as in the first century, and the compelling factors are not the same, either. Everything is different. The exact same strategy and methods of the first century won't work, but the principles will work.

Principles from Acts: Imposing Paul's Time Frame

Not too long ago, a missionary shared what happened during a luncheon that senior pastors had with the president of their association. One of the senior pastors asked the president about sending out missionaries. He stated that he only supports missionaries for two years. By then they should have a church planted and a national in charge. It sounds good on paper, but is it a sound universal policy to impose on your mission work? Many thoughts were racing through my mind, and, personally, I thought it an unsound policy.

In 1978 when I started full-time mission work, I moved to the state of Zacatecas in central Mexico. Zacatecas happened to be the least evangelized state in Mexico with less than 0.1 percent being evangelical. It was also one of the more religiously fanatical areas of Mexico, and the small evangelical population was persecuted and mistreated. Before my arrival, Gerry Witt, an American missionary, was killed there. After I moved there, I knew of one Mexican who had been beaten to death by a mob as the police watched because he had been passing out Christian tracts.

When I began mission work in Zacatecas, I thought it would only be to plant churches. I wouldn't realize until later that there was a bigger plan. God would use me to help change the hostile attitude that prevailed throughout the state toward evangelicals. Over the years, I gained favor with many government officials. At one time, I was in charge of distributing food, clothes, and other things donated to the fifty-six mayors of the state. All fifty-six mayors had to report to me to receive donations for their social programs. At that time I had connections high up in customs in Mexico City. They would give me permission to import donated items such as used clothes, food, medical equipment, and so forth. This meant that the mayors had to come to our church offices to request these items. The fact that Christians were meeting their needs caused them to reevaluate how they viewed evangelicals.

That is one of the many things that God did through me to help change the negative and hostile attitude toward evangelicals. By the time I left, we were respected by all of the political parties, including the communist groups, as well as many Catholic priests, police, and other authorities. This work may have been more important than the seven churches that I planted. My point is that if I had been obligated to leave after two years, that would have worked against what God wanted to accomplish. It took over twelve years to see things totally changed. It could not have been done in two.

I believe compelling factors should influence the length of time that a missionary stays in one place, and not a standard one-size-fits-all policy. For example, in Paul's case, he was strongly compelled to plant and move on because the nearest large city didn't have a church yet. Even with that in mind, some of Paul's churches may have fared better if he could have stayed longer. The church that I think was his most successful plant was Ephesus. It is stated in Acts 19:10 that all of Asia heard the word as a result of his ministry there. That is where Paul dedicated more time, around three and a half years. The two-year rule would have hindered Paul at Ephesus.

Each country, region, tribe, or people group will have its own positive and negative compelling factors. You will need to learn how to identify them and develop strategies and methods accordingly. If not, you will diminish your chances for success. If Paul had not seen the positive factor of the synagogue, for example, how do you think it would have affected his success? Let's say he viewed it as too hostile of a place and that it would just stir up trouble, so he would only evangelize the local gentiles. Without a doubt, this perspective would have affected the progress of his church-planting efforts in some way. It is important to learn to identify factors both negative and positive.

Identifying Compelling Factors

The following are a few examples of identifying positive and negative compelling factors from both missions history and my own experience. The stories of Hudson Taylor and Don Richardson are good examples. I have also included some personal stories from my past.

Hudson Taylor realized that European dress in the 1800s in China was a negative factor. He adopted Chinese dress and was able to travel freely without the unwanted attention that missionaries in European dress received.

Don Richardson, while ministering to unreached tribes in New Guinea, discovered the custom of giving a "peace child" to bring peace between warring tribes. When one of the warring tribes wanted peace, they would take one of their nursing babies and give it to the other tribe. As long as the peace child was alive, there was to be peace between the tribes. Before Don understood this concept, he had become discouraged in trying to make converts.

One of the highest cultural values of the tribe was being able to deceive someone. When Don shared the story of Jesus, Judas became their hero because he deceived Jesus. During that time, two of the tribes started fighting, and Don tried unsuccessfully to stop them. Finally, he told them that if they didn't stop their war he would leave. They didn't want him to leave because of the medicines and modern tools that he brought, so they promised to make peace. He wondered if it would last, since one of their highest values was to deceive. Wouldn't one tribe lull the other into a false sense of security and then attack?

What happened next astonished him. The two tribes met, and one tribe gave the other tribe a nursing baby, which they called the "peace child." The tribe giving the peace child would never attack because they dearly loved their children and wouldn't put the child's life in jeopardy. The tribe that received the child would never attack because it would be a disgrace not to honor the peace child treaty. This factor that Don had discovered would be used as a positive one to communicate the gospel. He preached Christ as God's peace child to mankind. Suddenly Judas became the villain because he betrayed a peace child. This became a factor that compelled the natives to listen to the Gospel, resulting in many conversions.

An example from my personal experience was showing

Christian movies, as I mentioned previously. There weren't any good TV shows on, and it was before VCRs. People would watch our movies because they didn't have color televisions yet. This approach was very effective for several years. A lot of missionaries, who couldn't learn Spanish well enough to plant churches, had movie ministries. In those days, if you announced a movie at church, you would have a full house.

In the "New Breed" chapter, I will talk of how the VCR became a powerful tool when it was new and how it helped in converting middle-class Mexicans. Someone identified that factor and made it into a compelling one, and many people were reached for Christ during that brief window of opportunity.

One of our strategies in Mexico is to start a work whenever a new colonia begins to develop. Mexican cities are divided into districts called *colonias*. We discovered that people in a new colonia are more receptive and less hostile than those in older colonias. Therefore, this factor compels us to start works in new colonias. We now try to buy land as soon as a new colonia is planned, and we might have a couple of lots purchased before a single house is built. The sooner, the better. We have discovered that if we were there before 80 percent of the people, the social dynamic changed. We are no longer the outsider trying to get into their old established colonias but are the group that is there before them. That changes everything.

In Mazatlán, Mexico, we began working in a new colonia twenty-five miles out of town. The way that most colonias begin is by a section being subdivided into lots, and then people begin to build before there are utilities. They then begin to pressure the government to provide the utilities. In this particular colonia, there was no electricity. I explained to the Mexican national that was working with us to plant the church that we needed to take advantage of the window of opportunity to show Christian movies. Soon the colonia would have electricity, televisions, and VCRs. The "no electricity" factor compelled us to get out the electric generator to show movies, and we were able to use them to evangelize quite effectively.

Another example of allowing compelling factors to influence your evangelism methods is in Mazatlán, which seems to be home to a lot of marital problems. There are probably a higher percentage of marital problems in Mazatlán than in most other areas of Mexico. That is nothing new, but what we have discovered is that people with these problems are open to receive help. We held a marriage seminar in the church and decided to place an ad in the local newspaper. To our surprise, more nonchurch people than church people showed up. Mazatlán's marital strife has thus become a compelling factor in our evangelism strategy.

Something else that we discovered in Mazatlán is that there are a lot of nonchurch attendees who like to read the Bible. We haven't developed a plan yet to take advantage of this, but down the road it may become a useful compelling factor.

One factor that I missed for a long time was the desire that professional and wealthy Mexicans had for socializing with Americans. It first came to my attention in the early 1980s. A local businessman offered to cash our U.S. checks for us, so every two or three weeks I would go by his office. Then I began to notice that he would send for me for a variety of reasons that I didn't think were very important. One day his chauffer came by and said that his boss wanted to know if I could come by and translate something for him. When I went by his office, he had a package of seeds from the United States and wanted me to translate the instructions. I hadn't figured out yet that he just wanted to be friends with the American. He was what is called an *"influyente,"* or an influential person in Mexico. He gained the title because of his wealth. I used to see police stopping by his place, and they would go away with some donation. I remember that one day he thought he saw a cop give him a mean look and put his hand on his gun. The next morning, he was at the police station. The chief assembled all of the officers to see if he could identify the culprit.

I didn't know that he was an influyente until after we became friends. I used to stop for coffee once a week and chat with him, and he always had his men wash my car each time. In 1981, my wife and I, along with our three-month-old daughter, were hit head-on on a highway just outside Fresnillo. Even though at that time I wasn't a real close friend of this influyente, when he heard about the accident, he sent his men out to guard my wrecked truck until friends retrieved the things in it. When I was in the hospital in a body cast, he heard that the drunk driver was trying to blame the accident on us, and he sent his lawyer to foil the attempt. After that, we became good friends.

On another occasion, when he heard that someone had come to my house to tell me I was targeted for assassination, he sent for me and asked me for the name of the man who had threatened me. I didn't know the name. A few years after, I myself would acquire the title of influyente, not because of my wealth but because I had gained the respect and friendship of many Mexican influyentes.

Another example happened when I went to a construction supply place, asked the owner for a discount on building supplies, and he agreed to it. Before I left, he said, "Come back and have a cup of coffee with me sometime." A couple of weeks later I returned and had a cup of coffee with him. I could tell that he enjoyed my visit, so every couple of weeks I would stop by for coffee. We talked politics, philosophy, business, history, and a hundred other subjects. One day he told me, "The priest comes to visit with me when he needs something, but you are the only one who visits me when you don't need something." This man was actually anti-American, but we became good friends. He would later help us out a lot on our projects for the poor. He still pays for feeding poor kids at two of our colonia projects.

One interesting case was the father of a lady who attended one of our churches. She and her husband lived next to the church, so we would stop by before services and visit with them. The lady's father lived with them and always seemed to be home when I stopped by. He was very anti-American, but he always engaged me in conversation. He had a Ford pickup truck, and if something was wrong with it, he would make comments about how the Americans made junk. "I want to buy a good truck, like a Datsun. Something that is built right, not like this American junk," he would say. I would agree and say, "Yeah, those Datsuns are a lot better than Fords. I'd like to own one myself." One day I mentioned to his daughter that maybe it would be better if I did not talk to her father since he was so hostile toward Americans. "Oh, no," she said, "you're the only Christian he will talk to. He won't even talk to the Mexicans."

There are many other examples such as these that I could

mention to describe the role of influyentes. This is one factor that I did not identify soon enough to maximize its potential. If I would have realized sooner that an American can socialize with the professional and wealthier classes and use it for evangelism, I could have made it a positive compelling factor. I just was not used to rich and powerful people wanting to be around me.

If I were in the Antioch church in the first century and I wanted to plant a church, it is likely that there would not be enough compelling factors to keep me in Antioch to do a new church plant. The compelling factors would be that, while there was already a church in Antioch, there were no churches in Corinth, Ephesus, Athens, Philippi, and Rome. The compelling factors would thus rule out staying in Antioch. I would be compelled to go to the next city and plant a church as quickly as possible.

The circumstances or compelling factors could also allow the church planter to leave prematurely. For example, if you explained to your converts that you have been with them for two years but the next big city down the road has not heard the good news yet, that would compel them to accept your departure.

A practical example of how circumstances can compel people to do things they normally would not do is when my family was hit head-on by a drunk driver. My wife and I were in the hospital. She had a broken arm, and all of her ribs on one side were broken as well as her pelvis. She also had multiple lacerations and a punctured lung. I was in a body cast with a crushed pelvis. We had no money in the bank and only had liability insurance on our truck. We did ask some friends to come in and fly our three-month-old daughter Amber to San Antonio, where she was placed in intensive care. We were broke and did not have ten dollars to our name. The liability insurance did cover $2,000 per person for injuries. With the low cost of treatment in Mexico, that amount would cover the hospital bill for a few days. So, we decided to tough it out and planned to have them move us to our apartment as soon as we were able. Fortunately, some Christians decided to come and get us. They sent in an airplane big enough to transport us out. If they had not done so, my wife would probably have died. The hospital in Mexico did not know that her lung was punctured and was filling up with blood. After she was operated on, she discovered that only 20 percent of people with her type of injuries survive.

When I knew we would be leaving soon, I sent for Mario, who was one of our converts. Mario had been a Christian a little over a year. I explained to him that we would be leaving in the next day or two and that I needed him to plant a church in the small community of Lobatos, forty-five miles from Fresnillo. We had just held a two-week medical clinic there, and Mario had helped me during that time. He accepted the responsibility but asked me, "What do I do?" I gave him a list of names of people who had responded to the invitation to receive Christ. I told him to visit these people and find out which ones were really converted, and see if one of them would open his or her home for a Bible study. The next day, we were taken to San Antonio, where we would spend three months hospitalized and under doctors' care. The fact that the planting had already begun with the medical caravan, that I was unable to continue to plant, and that I had no one else to do it became a compelling factor to allow a baby Christian to plant a church. That church is still going today.

Now, let us say that one day I decided to take some time off to relax, read some books, and pray. I would send for Mario and explain to him that I wanted some downtime and that I wanted him to go plant a church for me. How do you think he would react? Without a doubt he would have a bunch of reasons why there was nothing to compel him. Without a strong compelling factor, he would not be able to do it.

To further develop the concept of compelling factors, I will share some experiences I had in the United States. Perhaps by showing you these principals in the American culture, it will help you to discern compelling factors in other cultures.

During the turbulent sixties, along with the hippie movement and free love, the United States also experienced revival and a harvest of souls. One of the methods that was used by God to harvest many souls was the coffeehouse. Someone identified a compelling factor and invented a new ministry to take advantage of it. What was the compelling factor that gave birth to the coffee-house? It was a certain attitude that dominated the times. People wanted to debate ideas, philosophies, and even religion. They enjoyed challenging ideas and points of view in honest debate. They also liked to have their own ideas challenged as well. This desire to challenge and to be challenged opened the door for the "coffeehouse" ministry. At one time, all you had to do was hang out your shingle saying "Coffeehouse," and you would have a successful ministry. Thousands of coffeehouses sprang up all over the country. A multitude of souls were harvested. Most of us did not figure out the compelling factor dynamic; we just saw something that was working and copied it, which was a wise thing to do. You do not have to be the one to figure out all the compelling factors, but you need to be smart enough to follow those who do.

After a while, the social dynamic changed, however, and coffeehouses were no longer an effective instrument. Some people did not get it and continued to persist using yesterday's methods that no longer bore fruit. About the time when the coffeehouse was beginning to be unfruitful, the Full Gospel Businessman's Fellowship in our area decided to start a coffeehouse. They had seen and heard about the fruitfulness of these ministries and wanted to get in. Of course, they could not run one themselves, but they had the money, so they contacted some of us converted hippies to run their coffeehouse. The problem was, they waited too long, because the culture was changing once again, and the window of opportunity for winning souls with a coffeehouse ministry was fading fast. Most of us that were helping the Full Gospel Businessmen had already been active in the downtown coffeehouse in Peoria, Illinois. We had noticed a decline of fruitfulness already showing. The new coffeehouse was near Bradley University. We hung out our shingle and took to the streets with a handful of Gospel tracts and hearts full of zeal. However, the handwriting was on the wall. We had already heavily evangelized that area long before the new coffeehouse opened, and now the culture was in a new transition stage. We were not seeing people converted on the streets anymore.

During that time, the Full Gospel folks were stopping by to see how many converts we had made. Unfortunately, we did not have any although we were doing the same things that had been so fruitful two or three years before. We became concerned because the Full Gospel Businessmen were spending a lot of money in a high-dollar rent district. Finally, one of our workers made a convert. It was a young guy in his mid-twenties named JJ. After I met him and talked with him, I wondered if he really had been converted, but we needed someone and he was it. The Full Gospel Businessmen leaders had been bugging us to take one of the coffeehouse converts to give his testimony at one of their meetings. They scheduled JJ to come and give his testimony. Many of the Full Gospel Businessmen members were wanting to see the fruit of their giving. We used to joke about keeping JJ saved long enough to testify at the Full Gospel Businessmen's meeting. Just as we feared, shortly after testifying, he backslid.

After that, I suggested to the Full Gospel Businessmen leaders that they move the coffeehouse to a smaller and cheaper building that was for rent nearby. To my surprise, when we met with them, the young man that was living at the coffeehouse and serving as its director asked the men, "Did God tell you to rent this building or not?" What could they say? One of them spoke up and said, "Yes, God told us to rent this building." They were trapped. God had spoken and they could not do anything else. I did not think about talking to them about being good stewards of God's money. At that point, many of us quit working in the coffeehouse. They continued to waste money for a while but eventually had to shut down the fruitless ministry. This incident should not be taken as a criticism of the Full Gospel Businessmen. They have financed countless Christian projects and blessed multitudes. I share one incident where they missed the mark, as all ministries do on occasion.

Another brief window of opportunity during that time was the power of a good scientific argument that Jesus was who he said he was. With the openness of people wanting to debate and examine your ideas and have you challenge theirs, as well as the influence that modernism still had on our culture, God began to raise up people like Josh McDowell. Josh wrote the book *More Than a Carpenter* and the classic *Evidence That Demands a Verdict*. Josh and others like him would win thousands of converts using their scientific intellectual arguments. They had discovered the compelling factors of the times. People were open for debating ideas, and they wanted intellectual and scientific proof. During that time, my buddies and I all had a good scientific argument using the second law of thermodynamics, explaining that the laws of science support the creation theory. Soon the window would close as post-modernism began to take the place of modernism.

CHAPTER 2

Hudson Taylor Revisited

Presently, a lot of emphasis is placed on following Roland Allen's teachings concerning missions. I will say more about him in chapter 4. Allen certainly had some good things to teach and say about missions, and he was light-years ahead of his time on mission philosophy, but I find it a little troubling that very few have bothered to study any of Hudson Taylor's methods. Hudson Taylor was an English missionary in China during the nineteenth century. Although he did not write any books specifically on how to do missions, he was the most radical and revolutionary missionary of his time, and probably made the most radical changes in the history of missions. Roland Allen was involved in a very dysfunctional missionary system and society. He wrote books telling how missions should be done, but as far as I know, he never personally planted churches or practiced many of the principles himself. Instead, he remained a part of the same missions group that he found dysfunctional.

The main difference between Taylor and Allen is that even though they both saw serious problems in the way missions were done, Taylor *made* changes while Allen *wrote about* changes. Without a doubt, Allen was ahead of his time and had some excellent insights, but let us not forget that he did not put into practice all the methods that he wrote about. Therefore, it would be good to revisit Hudson Taylor and observe some of the things that he changed in missions that, at that time, were standard missions policy.

I think it is helpful to know that Taylor, when he began as a missionary, was part of a type of mission society that was similar to what Allen was involved in. We need to understand that people were simply working within their realm of understanding, and since many missionaries suffered great hardships for the sake of the Gospel, it is not wise to be too critical of missions at that time.

From reading the two volumes of Taylor's life's work, I have gleaned seven main changes that Taylor made in missions. Behind each one is a principle that we will identify. Some of the changes that occurred were considered so radical that, at one time, he lost much of his financial support from pastors and supporters in England. The European community and other missionaries in China harshly criticized Taylor.

The seven changes that Taylor made that upset so many people are the following:

1. He lived with the people. When Taylor arrived in China, the accepted practice was for missionaries to live in the European community located in the port cities. Taylor rented a house in the all-Chinese area of town. Although it had its challenges for a new missionary, Taylor began to see the advantages as well. This experience would also prepare him for his future work in inland China.

2. He adopted Chinese dress as well as amoral aspects of Chinese culture. At that time, all Western missionaries who went to China would continue to use Western dress. They had the attitude that their culture was superior to the Asian cultures. So, as missionaries arrived in China, they would continue to use Western dress and would stand out very much from the Chinese. Taylor, however, felt led to dress like the people to whom he was called to minister. A provoking question from a Chinese man caused him to make the change:

> One day a man asked Taylor to explain why he had buttons on the back of his coat! Taylor realized then that his Western-style dress was distracting his listeners from his message. He then decided to dress like a Mandarin Chinese teacher. He was amazed at

> how dressing like the Chinese allowed him to travel more freely and be accepted more readily by the people. Taylor's goal was not to have the Chinese become like English Christians, but to have them become Chinese Christians. (Curtis et al., p. 2)

Taylor even began to wear a ponytail. This move was so radical and offensive to the Western mindset that he was labeled a heretic. But as time went on, people noticed that he was able go into inland China and not draw any unwanted attention to himself. When the other Western missionaries would attempt to go from the port cities to inland China to share the Gospel, they would usually have trouble with the "rowdies." People looking for trouble would notice the Westerners, gather around, heckle their preaching, and at times stir up violence. Hudson Taylor, since he looked and dressed like the Chinese, could go in and preach; nobody thought anything of it. Over time, as the old-time missionaries began to notice this, many of them began to adopt the practice. Eventually, the pastors in England and other missions boards accepted it.

3. He abandoned the practice of limiting missions to port cities. When Taylor began as a missionary, the typical missions work in China was to set up a base in one of the port cities. "In those days, foreigners were not allowed into China's interior; they only were allowed in five Chinese ports. Hudson Taylor, however, was burdened for those Chinese millions who had never heard of Christ. Ignoring the political restrictions, he traveled along the inland canals preaching the gospel" (Curtis et al., p. 1). It was also convenient to remain in a port city. Missionaries would often live in mission compounds in these port cities, remaining disconnected from the Chinese people. In these compounds they would retain their Western lifestyle. Living in the port cities also provided a sense of security for the Westerners. If there was political unrest or any type of uprising, it was easy to get out of China. The journey to get back to the ports from the interior could take up to a month, depending on where in the interior one was. When Taylor founded the China Inland Mission (as the name indicates), he made a radical departure from the accepted missions practice of the time and began to concentrate mission work in the completely unevangelized cities of inland China. Over time, his mission sent hundreds of missionaries to the large cities in inland China, as well as to the mountains to evangelize the indigenous tribes. By 1895, the mission had 641 missionaries. At the time of his death in 1905, the China Inland Mission had 125,000 Chinese Christians. This was accomplished in a country that was entirely hostile to all foreigners.

4. He lowered the bar. When he founded the China Inland Mission, Taylor was receptive to people with little formal education. He looked for men and women with aptitudes in evangelism and learning the Chinese language. He did not only look for professional ministers. No other mission societies had opened the door for the rank-and-file layperson with little education to be sent out as missionaries. Whenever we release the laypeople, we release the power of the Holy Spirit. Read the history of the Methodist and the Pentecostal movements. The Methodists were lay driven. The Methodist church became the largest in the United States at one time. After they went to seminary-trained pastors, they began to decline in number. Hudson Taylor lowered the bar as far as man's standards are concerned. If you study the history of the China Inland Mission, you will find many great missionaries that probably would not have been accepted in other organizations.

5. He offered no guaranteed salaries but faith-based missions. Missionaries were not guaranteed a salary. Being accepted by the typical missions society guaranteed the missionary some financial security. Mission societies would often borrow money when donations were down to cover the salaries of their missionaries. Not having to worry about finances took a big load off the missionary. However, Taylor was vehemently opposed to mission societies going into debt. He would not do so. Therefore, all China Inland Missionaries had to accept this new policy of trusting God to supply the needed funds. He would be tested many times on this point.

6. He accepted women as missionaries, not limiting them to traditional roles. Taylor's policy toward women was a radical departure from accepted missions practice and one of the changes that sparked a lot of criticism. At that time, women were accepted as missionaries in the traditional role of schoolteacher or orphanage worker. Taylor not only recognized women as full-fledged missionaries but also sent them to inland China. He opened the door for women when it was not popular to do so. Both society and the church disapproved and did not disguise their contempt for him. Today, women's rights are such a part of Western culture that anything that is considered an advancement for women will generate instant support in our society. Taylor had no support. For the most part he stood alone and weathered the storm. Of course, history has vindicated Taylor and condemned his detractors.

7. Decisions were to be made on the field in China. This premise would be the guiding principle for the China Inland Missions. Boards in England controlled other mission societies; men who had never been missionaries, who did not speak a foreign language, and had no understanding of the cultures where they had missionaries made decisions. Taylor's way was a major departure from standard missions practice. Veteran missionaries would now decide policies. In the beginning, it would be Taylor himself making all the decisions, but as the China Inland Mission grew, he gladly delegated the task to other veteran missionaries. He established a board in England to handle affairs such as collecting funds, bookkeeping, and informing supporters of activities in China. As the China Inland Mission grew, Taylor formed a China board consisting of battle-tested veteran missionaries.

The English board would soon decide that they needed more control over affairs in China would challenge this policy. Remember that, at this time, missionaries and the European community in China as well as other societies in England were harshly criticizing Taylor. He was criticized for not being university trained and for not being ordained. Before he founded the China Inland Mission, he had resigned from the mission society that sent him, so he was branded as a man connected to no one, recognized by no one, and fanatical. After adopting Chinese dress and requiring China Inland Missionaries to do the same, he was despised even more. The China Inland Mission was made fun of as the "ponytail mission," since Taylor and the China Inland Missionaries grew ponytails like the Chinese they were ministering to.

With all this criticism constantly agitating the waters, when several of his own missionaries began to complain about the way he was running things and refused to wear Chinese dress, the board in England felt the pressure as well. With the China Inland Mission still in its infant stage, the English board tried to take control. I am sure Taylor felt the pressure. But, to his credit, he held his ground and refused to change this important principle that would help the China Inland Mission become the biggest and most effective missions group of its time.

Without doubt, this change is still the least practiced today, but to their credit, many missions organizations have made adjustments in this area. However, there are some who still do not get it. Some mission agencies, church denominations, mission task forces, and mission partnerships continue to follow the old model, thinking they are smart enough to do so because of the many books on missions they have read. Some are making major mistakes and do not even realize it. I know of one group that has placed people over entire nations or groups of nations, and the person in charge makes no attempt to learn the language. I know of men who have worked for years in the same country and plan on continuing to do so for years to come, but have never cracked a book or enrolled in a course to learn the language. How can you say, "I'm giving my life to Latin America," for example, and not consider it important or an obligation to learn the language?

Translating Taylor's Principles to the Missions of Today
It is unfortunate for us that Taylor did not write a book on how to do missions since he is the one who actually practiced his methods. But one thing we can receive from the two-volume book about his life is his passion for missions. I believe that at times there is too much focus on missionary methods and not enough focus on passion. When the going gets tough, you may have the right methods, but if you do not have passion, you will not be able to make it through rough times when your life is threatened as a missionary, or when you are suffering serious financial problems. Passion can get you through those things. Taylor had very good philosophies and methods for ministry as well as a strong passion that he instilled in

the other missionaries that joined the China Inland Mission.

How, then, do the changes that Hudson Taylor made in the 1800s translate into twenty-first century practice? Today's world is drastically different from that of Hudson Taylor's and Roland Allen's time, and there is no standard answer as to how we should adapt to other cultures. Each country and culture needs to be studied and analyzed. Prayerful discernment should be sought for how to adapt to each new culture.

I once saw a news report about the U.S. Special Forces troops that were sent to Afghanistan for the purpose of traveling throughout the country to evaluate the people's needs and then to report on any urgent problems such as starvation. None of them wore army uniforms. Not only were they dressed in civilian clothing, including turbans like those worn by the locals, but they also wore beards as is the custom there. If the U.S. government can figure out such a simple concept, then the church should not have any trouble. Since the 1800s, the East has moved toward the West, and although the differences in standards are not nearly as obvious as in China in the 1800s, they do exist.

In some ways, the Western mentality has not changed much. For example, even though Latin America and Mexico have a more conservative dress standard than the United States, many people seem unaware of it. Others feel no obligation to conform to Latin standards when visiting or doing mission work. In Mazatlán, we host many short-term ministry teams. To their credit, many of them ask about dress standards. I explain to them that as foreigners in Mexico, we already stand out. Why do something that will make us stand out even more, like dress in clothing that is more revealing than what their local culture accepts?

I lived in central Mexico in the state of Zacatecas for seventeen years. The standards there are different than those in Mazatlán. At times factors other than morals (such as the climate) affect dress standards. In the high mountains of Fresnillo, Zacatecas where I lived, no one wore shorts. The climate was very dry, and in the summer it would often get hot during the day, but it always cooled off at night. I only wore shorts for playing sports, which was the norm. It was not my job as a gringo to change local standards. I have been away from Zacatecas for seven years now, and the culture has changed. You now see some locals wearing shorts during the summer months.

In Mazatlán, the locals wear shorts but not year-round, usually from June through September. Following the local standard, I do not normally wear shorts during the winter months, either. As Hudson Taylor found, it is our job to blend in, not to stand out.

Let us identify the principles behind Hudson Taylor's methods and strategy so that we can apply them to our missions work today:

1. What is the principle behind living outside the European community in the less safe Chinese neighborhood? Relationship. Connect with people you are called to minister to. Get to know them, socialize with them, learn how they think, and become friends with them.

2. What is Hudson Taylor's principle in taking on Chinese dress as well as embracing all positive amoral aspects of their culture? This says that you are not only willing to be friends with them but that you also want to become one of them. It speaks of respect for them and their culture. One mistake that many missionaries made was not recognizing and embracing positive things in the cultures where they ministered. One easy-to-grasp example of embracing positive cultural aspects is the *quinceñera* practiced in Mexico. The quinceñera is a special party for girls when they turn fifteen, and it is a major event. It is a coming-of-age party that resembles a wedding without the groom. Both of my daughters had quinceñeras. I would not have considered not doing so. It is a very positive event. The Mexican Christians have contextualized it, and it is often held at church with a Bible-centered focus.

3. What is the principle behind not limiting his work to the ports? You cannot let circumstance alone dictate where you do missions work. When Taylor arrived in China, missionaries were restricted to working in five port cities. With the compelling factor of millions of unevangelized Chinese in the interior, he was compelled to go there. There were plenty of reasons not to go to inland China. The government did not permit it, it could be dangerous, travel was difficult, and Europeans had no guarantee of protection as in the port cities.

You should not choose where to do missions based solely on ease of travel, convenience, cost, and safety. If these are the only factors directing your decisions, you are probably not being led by the Spirit. Many churches that want to work in Mexico choose to go to the U.S.–Mexican border. Very often such a decision is based solely on the things I have mentioned. Am I saying these things should not be considered? No. Not at all. They should be a part of the equation, but not the only dictating factor of where you do missions.

In 1999, we sent a team to Juarez, across the border from El Paso, to plant a church. We have decided not to send any more church-planting teams to the border at this time. We are open if in the future God wants to direct us to do so. The Juarez team soon found out how different things were and that the Mazatlán methods didn't always work. For example, in Mazatlán we would hold small mini-crusades in the different colonias. Our team tried that in Juarez, and it didn't work. They informed me that people wouldn't attend unless something was given away, such as clothes or a bag of groceries. There were so many short-term church groups that had held campaigns and drawn crowds by giving something away that people now expected it. If you didn't have something to give them, they wouldn't come out. The team leader then went to scout out a fairly new colonia and told me there were already seven small churches started. Halleluiah. Isn't that what we want? More churches? But rather than trying to plant another small church there, let's find some places to work where there aren't that many churches. After a while, our team targeted the *cholos* (gangs) for evangelism. Even though there were churches all over, none were reaching the tattooed, baggy-pants kids.

Sometimes, I get letters from churches that have been working at the border, asking what I think about the pastor or church they are helping in Mexico. When I know the person they are helping, I tell them the pastor is a good guy. I would not feel right saying, "There are better places to work. Come on down and help us." Not everyone who goes to the border does so because it is more convenient, easier, or cheaper. For many, those are the only contacts they have.

Remember this principle: Mission work is not about you. It is about the nationals. If your missions work is only about you and your people getting blessed, or your youth feeling good about helping the poor, then your focus is wrong. It is not about your being blessed but about *their* being blessed. Consider cost, transportation, distance, and so forth, but don't allow them to be the only compelling factors. We want you to be blessed on your mission trip, but don't make it a requirement that you feel blessed because of what you have done. Sometimes we go to new areas and are not well received, and maybe we won't feel blessed, but someone has to go there and break ground.

It is easier to recruit short-term teams to Mazatlán than it is to central Mexico. In Mazatlán, during the afternoon break, you can hang out at the beach. In central Mexico, there is not much to do on your break. Now, I can be upset about the state of the church, sending short-term missions teams to the "easy" places, or I can be proactive and turn it into a positive thing. After a church has come a few times to Mazatlán, I begin to tell them about the opportunities in central Mexico. We now have a few churches choosing the less attractive option and going to central Mexico. One group that went was blessed and has committed to return there instead of returning to Mazatlán.

4. What principle lies behind Taylor's lowering of the bar? How much evidence do we need to figure out that seminary-trained professionals are not the driving force of the church? Christian Swartz, in his study of churches around the world, revealed some interesting things. In his book *Natural Church Development*, he states that the seminary-trained pastors are a negative in church growth. The majority of churches with a seminary-educated pastor were either not growing or shrinking. I didn't say it. He did.

I mentioned the Methodist movement in the United States in the 1800s. The Methodists were the first to arrive at the new frontier communities. Nearly all of their pastors were lightly educated laymen, yet they conquered the Wild West. After they grew to be the largest denomination in the United States, they began to install more and more seminary-trained pastors. The denomination also began to decline. They are not the powerhouse that you read about in the autobiography of Peter Cartwright, one of their more famous circuit riders. Am I saying we don't need education and training for our pastors? Not at all. But I am saying we don't need that many with seminary training. Later I'll explain our philosophy and strategy for training workers. The principle is to look for gifts before titles. The Holy Spirit gives gifts and a calling. Seminary can't give any gifts or passion. Taylor learned to look for passion and gifts before education.

5. What is the principle behind not offering guaranteed salaries, because Taylor's was a faith-based mission. The principle: God is our provider and will meet our needs. Not only did Taylor not guarantee salaries, he didn't allow the China Inland Missionaries to make overt appeals for funds as other societies would do. The China Inland Mission would be a testimony of God's provision and would lay the spiritual foundation for the modern "new breed" missionary to build on. It is always easier when you can look back at those who have gone before you. You can say, "God took care of them, and He will take care of me as well." This will be a major challenge for those coming from an Evangelical, non-Pentecostal background. Even modern Pentecostals are looking more colonial in their need to make appeals for funds.

Recently, I was involved with a pastor wanting to come to Mexico as a full-time missionary. He installed a pastor and turned his church over. The denominational leader then made him take a psychological test. Afterward they required him to raise more than twice the support he needed to get started. I wrote them a letter explaining that they were looking very colonial. I shared briefly about faith-based missions and the success they have had, and the importance of building on those successes.

6. What is the principle behind Taylor's policy toward women? The principle is that, in Christ, there is neither male nor female. It has more to do with your passion and gifts than your gender. Of course, in modern Western culture, the equality of women is constantly trumpeted. If you are perceived as antiwoman or an oppressor of women, our society will eat you alive. This is the area that needs less emphasis since we now have more female missionaries than male. Thousands of women have taken advantage of the opportunity first made possible by Hudson Taylor. That is one door that will never be closed.

7. What principle lies behind the approach that decisions be made on the field? This is the one change that will be resisted more than any of the others. How do you tell someone who has studied missions, has a degree in missiology, and has read all the books on missions that he or she is not the most qualified person to run missions? Running missions from the United States or England has not been as fruitful as it could have. How do you convince the stateside board that they need a field manager (missionary) who speaks the language, knows the culture, and understands the bad things that can happen when money is not used properly? Giving up power is one of the hardest things for us to do. We like to have control. And when money is involved, especially *our* money, we sometimes feel like we deserve power. Accepting this change also requires humility and an in-check ego. Taylor had to fight the battle for on-the-field-control when the England China Inland Mission board felt like they should take control. He won the battle, and the China Inland Mission experienced incredible growth and success.

Today, men and women feel more qualified to run missions from the United States because of the numerous books they have read about missions. Some people, after having read all the missions books, develop a certain arrogance that I find nauseating. Even though they have never been a missionary, planted a church, suffered hardship for the Gospel, or lived in a foreign country, they seem to know all about missions. Whenever they open with the question "Are you raising up nationals?" I know they have read books about the colonial missionaries and assume you may be one of them. My answer is usually, "Of course I'm raising up nationals. Is there any other way to do it?" This ain't your Daddy's Oldsmobile, and we ain't colonial missionaries. I am amazed that church movements that think they are "cutting-edge" still put people in charge of foreign missions who don't speak the language and have never lived in a foreign country.

In the late 1980s, I was visiting in California. A man I had just met invited me to the new church he was starting the following Sunday. I was there in his first Sunday service and was amazed to see what I estimated to be more than five hundred people in the school gymnasium. The home church, which had several thousand members, had encouraged people to leave and become part of the new church. The short story is that this new church plant of five hundred grew backward, and, a few years later, the pastor closed down the church and returned to the original church. Sometime after that, he was put in charge of world missions in his denomination. His job was to get missions going in the rest of the world.

If some of our missions programs were businesses, the CEOs would have all been fired or be doing hard time for mismanagement. Maybe we need to start a Bad Missions Police Force and serve warrants to dumb gringos. The evidence would be overwhelming, and our conviction rate would be high. To be released from the dumb missions prison, one would have to learn a foreign language. If you really want to be cutting-edge and do missions the new way, first you'll have to stop putting the type of people in charge that I have mentioned.

What Makes for a Qualified Missionary Today?
Today we have many advantages over our predecessors. We can study their history, as well as read hundreds of books on missions and how to do missions. However, those things cannot replace the wisdom and knowledge that come from living for years in a foreign country and learning the language and the culture.

The following is a list of things I believe you need in order to identify a qualified person, able to run and oversee your missions programs:

1. Several years' experience as a missionary living in a foreign country.
2. Fluency in the language. He or she should be able to preach and teach in the language of the country where he or she ministers.
3. Is he or she what I call "culturally fluent"? Can, and does, the person give you cultural tips? For example, I have explained many times to visiting American pastors that in Mexico, when you enter a room, you shake hands with everyone and when you leave, you shake hands again. In

Mexico, if you want to shun someone, you don't shake his or her hand.

4. Has he or she planted several churches—more than one or two? The exception would be if the person has a healthy, good-size church that is sending out nationals to plant churches.

5. Are the churches he or she planted under national leadership? Do the nationals make their own decisions? Does the missionary still live in the area where the church (churches) is located? Would they do as well if the missionary left, or are they dependent on him or her?

6. Are the churches financially independent? Does the national pastor receive money from the missionary? Does the church need outside support? If the missionary has done his or her job, there shouldn't be any national pastors or workers receiving outside support. That is not to say that you can never come back and help the church on some project or special need.

7. Have any of the churches established by the missionary planted other churches?

8. Has the missionary connected with the community? Is he or she respected by the people, both the churched and the secular? Normally, when someone learns and adapts to the culture, people respond by accepting and respecting the missionary. Even though you don't speak the language, if you are observant, you can tell whether he or she is well received in the community. The exception might be a very hostile environment, but even then, in most cases, when the missionary is on site for several years, he will gain the respect of the community. I started out in a very hostile area of Mexico. Even though I was getting death threats from religious fanatics and the communists, I had earned the respect of the community and government officials.

9. Has he or she become "one of them"? Like Hudson Taylor adopting Chinese dress to become more like the people, has this missionary become a part of the people

group where he or she ministers? Do the national pastors and leaders like to hang with the missionary? If he or she is helping them out financially, of course they'll want to. The true test is if the nationals have no financial incentive and they still want to socialize with the missionary. Of course, we'll always be foreigners, but it is possible to be so accepted that at times the nationals will actually forget that the missionary is an outsider. When this happens, it puts the missionary in a unique position to listen in as both pastors and laypeople express their true feelings about the Americans who come to minister among them. I have had the opportunity to be hanging with nationals when the conversation turns to the gringos that minister in Mexico. Some of (not all) our pastors and missions leaders don't have a clue about how the nationals really see them and the way they handle finances.

The following is one example of how gringos who don't speak the language or understand the culture can mess things up and not even realize it. One pastor, whom I'll call Doug, pastors a church in the United States. He was asked by his denomination to work in missions in Latin America. The missions leader in Doug's denomination didn't want to send in Westerners to plant churches, so he had to find a national to plant under his church banner. The man whom Doug found was not yet equipped to plant a church, so he moved him to the United States where he could be further discipled. I had just gotten to know Doug and I wanted to scream out "Doug, what are you doing?!" But having just met him, I didn't think it wise to tell him he had done one of the stupidest things I have heard of. Eventually, they felt that the national, whom I'll call Juan, was trained enough to send him back. Here is the short version: Juan did not stay in Latin America. He is now back in the United States and has no plans of returning.

I did get to know Doug, and, since then, he has taken two short-term ministry teams to Mazatlán. On his second visit to Mazatlán, I felt like we were good friends and that I could ask the tough question.

"Doug," I asked, "why in the world would you move a national to the United States? That was the dumbest thing you could have done. If you would have had a five-minute conversation with me, I could have given you a list of reasons why not to do it." Doug explained that he had called the national missions director in the United States, whom I'll call Ed, and he had told him to take Juan to the States to train him.

After I got to know Doug, I realized that he was a pretty sharp guy and he did the right thing in asking his missions leader what to do. How was he to know the leader didn't really understand the situation? Ed had read all the books on missions. Roland Allen's books are the ones that the director recommends the most. With all the knowledge that he gained from missions books (most of them are good reading), in the end he was a dumb gringo who made a dumb decision that totally changed the life of a man who may have done well planting churches if better decisions had been made. To this day, I don't think Ed understands the consequences his bad decision had on the life of another. For a while, Juan had stopped attending church. Chances are he will never plant a church or leave the good life in the United States. Of course, there are a few exceptions where it will work out to take a national to the States, but someone who doesn't speak the language probably won't know when it is not appropriate.

To be highly effective in the twenty-first century, we can't continue to do missions the old way, running things with men and women who are not fluent in the language or culture. Nor will the old type of missionary be effective running missions. The new missionary with the nine characteristics I have mentioned will make our missions and missions boards cutting-edge. Continue to read all the good books on missions, but seek out the type of person I mentioned for consultation and advice.

Another common mistake that gringos (who work in Mexico) make is to put Mexican Americans in charge. (I am referring to second-, third-, and fourth-generation Americans of Mexican descent.) I think there are two reasons why they do this. First, the leaders aren't bilingual, and having a Mexican American involved makes it easier for them. They don't have to learn Spanish because the Mexican American becomes their interpreter. Second, they assume that Mexican nationals automatically accept Mexican Americans as their own. That is a natural but mistaken assumption. Before living in Mexico for several years, I assumed the same thing. I was surprised when I learned otherwise.

The first time this Mexican American issue came to my attention was in Fresnillo in the early 1980s. That year, we had two marriage seminars, one by a missionary and another by a Mexican American couple from California. Later, when I met with our national leaders, I mentioned that we needed to plan another marriage seminar and asked them whom they wanted to invite. Frank, who taught the first seminar, was a veteran missionary who spoke Spanish with a terrible accent. He was always making gender mistakes when he spoke. In Spanish, nouns have a feminine or masculine gender, and he was always getting them mixed up. For example, instead of saying "la casa," he would say "el casa." I was sure they wouldn't want Frank back. "Do you think we should invite Hernandez for another seminar?" I asked. "No", they said, "We want the gringo to come back." I was dumbfounded. "Are you sure?" I asked. They were firm in their convictions. As I learned more about the culture, I realized it had nothing to do with looking up to gringos and an attitude that Americans are superior in some way. They sensed something that I didn't notice at that time. They sensed an attitude of superiority in the Mexican American that they didn't like. The gringo loved the Mexicans and had a desire to serve them and to bless them, and they knew it. I have since learned that if it had been the gringo with the attitude, they would have rejected him instead. Mexican Americans have no automatic advantage with Mexican nationals. Many Mexican Americans are not aware of this.

A few years ago, I was in a meeting with several American pastors in Mexico. One of the American leaders always had a Mexican American pastor accompany him when he visited Mexico. I mentioned that the Mexican nationals didn't see him as a Mexican but as an American. A brief time of laughter followed, and later on I heard a few jokes about the Mexican gringo. They thought I was crazy.

I thought I had a good grasp of the Mexican culture, but I was surprised by something that happened after that. Oscar de la Hoya, the great Mexican American boxer, was scheduled to defend his title against a Puerto Rican boxer. Mexicans are not especially fond of Puerto Ricans, and I was sure that they would be rooting for their fellow Mexican. With my understanding of the culture, I was convinced they would support Oscar de la Hoya. To my surprise and shock, I couldn't find anyone rooting for Oscar—not one Mexican. I couldn't believe it. I asked our worship leader who he was going for. He is a very committed Christian, and I was sure he was for Oscar. "I'm with the Puerto Rican," he told me. But, I protested, "Oscar is Mexican." My worship leader informed me that Oscar is American. A year earlier Oscar beat Chavez, a legendary Mexican boxer, and they never forgave him. Even before beating the Mexican champion, de la Hoya was never embraced by the Mexican nationals. Gringos and Mexican Americans, please understand this point.

Work Cited

Curtis, Ken, Beth Jacobson, Diana Severance, Ann T. Snyder, and Dan Graves. "Hudson Taylor: A Heart for China's Millions." *Glimpses* 47 Christian History Institute).

CHAPTER 3

A New Kid on the Block: The New Breed

W ithout a doubt, Hudson Taylor was the prototype of what I refer to here as the "new breed" missionary. However, he did not start from zero. I believe he built upon what he learned from his contact with and knowledge of the new breed missionaries of his time.

One of these missionaries was George Muller. Muller is traditionally known for his work with orphans and his trusting God to meet his needs. In his earlier years, Muller had a burden for the Jews and began to associate with the London Jews Society. He severed his ties with them over two points that he consciously objected to. The first was the requirement to be ordained by the Church of England. The second was the control the missions board wanted to exercise over him. The new missions thinking was beginning to emerge. Muller intuitively knew that missionaries, to be effective, needed to be at liberty to be led by the Holy Spirit and not controlled by missions boards. In 1836, he founded the Scriptural Knowledge Institute for Home and Abroad. His ministry, among several other things, would support many missionaries. He would apply the "new missions principle" of supporting missionaries without trying to exercise control over them.

At one point, when Hudson Taylor had been branded a man

connected to no one, not recognized by anyone, unordained, and reckless, Muller became his main supporter. Because of these criticisms, Taylor had lost most of his financial support. I am sure that this contact and fellowship with Muller influenced his thinking in missions.

Another new-thinking, new breed missionary who emerged in the early 1800s was Anthony Norris Groves. Groves, desiring to go out as a missionary, planned on joining the Church Missionary Society. However, when informed that he would have to be ordained in the Lutheran Church or Church of England, he could not consciously agree with that requirement, so he planned to join as a layman. When he was told that only ordained ministers could administer the Lord's Supper, he resigned from the Church Missionary Society. He then went out as a missionary to Baghdad without a guaranteed salary, trusting in the Lord to supply his needs. Groves was an incredible progressive, new missions thinker.

After working several years in Baghdad, Groves made a trip to India to encourage missionaries and mission societies. He desired to see unity among the different missions societies, built around the need to reach the multitudes in India. This was fairly well received. But when Groves tried to share some of the new missions thinking that he had developed, things began to change. When he pointed out that the Europeans needed to mix more with the natives, he was seen as attacking them. He suggested to them that, whenever a European missionary traveled to preach the Gospel, he take six natives with him, with whom he would eat, drink, and sleep as he traveled. His desire to help the missions societies with his new missions thinking was not well received by the colonial missionaries. Opposition grew, and he was excluded from fellowship and called an enemy and a danger to the work. Groves then settled in India, where he continued to practice his new missions principles.

One thing that Groves had yet to learn would concern giving salaries to natives. That practice was something that was now common in colonial missions, and Groves was planning to continue the practice. Had it not been for the spirituality of Aroolappen, a native worker that he was sending out to preach the Gospel, he may not have learned this important concept. Aroolappen refused any salary because the people, he said, would not cease to tell him that he preached because he was hired. What an incredible Christian to be able to turn down financial security! As a result of this experience, Groves would observe that salaries and money kept the Indian people dependant on the Europeans. He understood that even though the typical indigenous Christian preferred a provision and ease, to be independent, he had to be "thrown" to God. Groves became a close friend of Muller, and I am sure both of them exercised a profound influence on Hudson Taylor.

Taylor was the prototype of the new missionary. He was the one who made the radical changes that the new breed missionary would build on. I have not done a detailed study on missions from Taylor's time to the present. However, I have observed, over the last twenty-five years, the accomplishments of those I call the "new breed." Who is the new breed modern missionary, and what are the new breed accomplishments?

Discovering the New Breed

In the early eighties, I attended a world missions conference in Guadalajara, Mexico. The conference was sponsored by Baptist and Presbyterian churches. I had the opportunity to meet and have a couple of meals with Don Richardson, the author of *The Peace Child*. Don is probably one of the most effective Evangelical missionaries of our time.

What I remember most, however, is one of the workshops I attended. The gentleman who conducted the workshop was a Presbyterian. In his workshop, he pointed out that in 1900, over 90 percent of the Protestants in Mexico were made up of mainline traditional churches—Baptist, Presbyterian, Methodist, Congregational, and so forth. By the 1980s, the mainline churches only made up 10 percent of the Protestant community. The other 90 percent were nontraditional groups, mostly Pentecostals. Then the workshop leader asked, "Why have they grown so much and we haven't?" I guess he thought that all of us were from traditional Evangelical churches. A time of discussion followed his challenging question. The conclusion that I have come to is that it is the fruit of the new breed missionary. Many people are still unaware of the great accomplishments of this little-noticed group.

This point came to my attention once again when I later attended the pastors' conference that I mentioned in chapter 1. One day, the senior pastors were invited to have lunch with the president of their association of churches. After the meal, the pastors were invited to ask any questions that they wanted. One of the questions was what his views were on sending out missionaries. His reply was that he would only support a missionary for two years. He went on to say that the Achilles heel of evangelical missionaries had been their inability to raise up and turn over a work to nationals. He felt that somehow, by their being supported from the outside, it contributed to the problem. I wanted to tell him, "You're looking at the wrong group of missionaries. Haven't you noticed in Mexico the numerous Pentecostal, Charismatic, and other nontraditional church movements? Ask the question, 'Where did they come from?' It isn't the fruit of the mainline Evangelical missionaries. It was the work of nontraditional, mostly Pentecostal missionaries."

I knew that the president of the church association had formed his policy as a reaction to the Evangelical missionaries. In my mind I was screaming, "Study the other missionaries, the new breed,' and learn from them! Build on their example!" Then I reminded myself that he probably is unaware of them, for the most part.

As I have already stated, I have not researched missions since the Azusa Street Revival to the present. I am sharing my personal observations of men and women who began as missionaries during the 1950s and 1960s and have been referring to them as the "new breed." A second group began to arrive in the 1970s and early 1980s, which I will call the "second wave." The second wave was a product not only of Pentecostal influence but also of the Charismatic and Jesus movements. They would follow the trail blazed by the new breed, learning from them and building on their example. However, they would be different and be used by God to accomplish things that the new breed had not.

The new breed, for the most part, was the product of the Pentecostal movement. As the movement grew and progressed, it weakened the barrier between the clergy and laity. The spiritual wall of separation between professional minister and layperson was beginning to crack. This would pave the way for the emergence of the new breed. Once again the bar was lowered. Unfortunately, some Pentecostal denominations now began to do missions in a more colonial way. They would also raise the bar for educational requirements.

Who were these new breeds? What did they look like? What were the things that distinguished them? What did they do differently? There is no one set answer that will fit all, but I will describe some of the main traits that I have noticed.

Trait 1: They were men and women with passion for world missions

The battle cry of the Pentecostals was "Go ye into all the world." I was able to witness some of this passion in my early years on the mission field. Before I left for the mission field, I had accumulated a few rental properties with the plan of supporting myself from the income. To make a long story short, God showed me that this was not His plan, but mine. I sold the properties, paid off the bank notes, bought an almost-new pickup, and found myself without money. I would have to go by faith. When I arrived in central Mexico, I had very little committed support. Some missionaries I had met invited me to a mission conference that several small Pentecostal churches held every year. I felt a little funny going because I wasn't a classic Pentecostal. When we arrived at the church in Louisiana Bayou country, I felt like I was at someone else's family reunion. The people were wonderful and friendly, but it seemed I was the only one who wasn't known by everyone. The church provided room and board for the three-day conference. Otherwise, I wouldn't have been able to go. I only had enough gas money to get to the conference, so I needed God to provide for the return trip. I didn't tell anyone about my need. So, it would have to be God.

I will never forget the first night at the conference. I would witness the Pentecostal passion for missions firsthand. We sang and worshiped for a good while. Afterward, an offering was taken up for missions. One of the pastors preached, and I thought the service was over. Then the host pastor came to the pulpit and said, "Our first special need is a new truck for Brother So-and-So. Who can help us out?" (Back then, in the Pentecostal circles, everyone was addressed as Brother or Sister.) Someone yelled out, "I'll give two hundred dollars." "OK, Brother John for two hundred dollars. Who else?" "I'll give one hundred dollars." Another, "I'll give five hundred dollars." A pastor announced, "My church will give a thousand." In a few minutes, they had raised several thousand dollars. I couldn't believe what I was seeing. I had never witnessed anything like it. That was the passion that produced the new breed missionary. The group with whom I have been involved for twenty years claims to have embraced the best from both the Evangelical and Pentecostal camps. But I have never seen the passion that I witnessed that night in my own group, though I have desired to see it.

What happened that first night would be repeated the next two days at the morning, afternoon, and evening services. The conference ended Saturday night. Jack Wells, a pastor I had met at the conference, asked me if I would preach at his church in Franklin, Louisiana. I gladly accepted the invitation. My wife and I followed him home that night and stayed with him at his house next to the small Pentecostal church. The next morning, after worship, when the offering was taken up, Brother Jack announced, "Now we're going to take up an offering for Brother Fred." I would soon learn that their passion for missions presented no problems in a second offering. God had also supplied the needed funds for us to return to Mexico. I then preached and afterward turned the microphone back over to Brother Jack. Then, to my astonishment, Brother Jack said, "Brother Fred doesn't have enough support. I need people to make a monthly commitment beyond your tithe for one year." I was amazed. A second offering was taken, and now monthly support was being requested for a Brother whom none of them had ever seen before. This was a small working-class church, so when one hundred fifty dollars for monthly support was raised, we were very happy. Brother Jack, as time went by, would promote us in other churches. He had been a traveling evangelist for years and was highly regarded in many churches.

Over the next few years, I would preach in several Pentecostal churches in Louisiana. My preaching style was not very Pentecostal, but they seemed to like it and take to us. One pastor kept asking me to come for a month. He said he would line up a different place for me to preach every night, and each church would take up a special offering. Finally, I told him I would come for two weeks. True to his word, he had a service scheduled every night at a different church, with two churches on Sunday. I was quite tired after two weeks and very glad not to have taken up his offer of a one-month preaching marathon.

I had experienced Pentecostal passion for missions. It would propel them to become the dominant church movement in the third world. I thank God that I was able to witness it. There are more stories I could share. Later televangelists would take advantage of their passion for giving and build big ministries. Because of the way televangelists constantly cried and asked for money, many newer movements overreacted and now hardly ever receive a second offering for missions at a meeting. Many pastors are afraid to do so.

Trait 2: They were independent.
They would often work with an established missionary for a season and then launch out on their own. Their passion would lead them to unevangelized areas where they would start a work. Sometimes they were independent to a fault, but they got the job done. Not having a missions board telling them what to do allowed them to be more effective.

Trait 3: Most were not sent out by or connected to a missions board.
If they were connected to a missions group, it was often a group started by a new breed missionary. I think that is one reason why many people don't know about them. Independent churches that had no mission boards often sent them out. That makes it hard to collect information about them. We don't even know how many there were. I have the privilege of knowing a handful. But the Lamb of God knows them all, and many will shine as the sun on that great day.

Trait 4: They went by faith, often beginning without enough financial support.
Their passion for world missions and winning the lost caused them

to go forward, at times suffering financial hardships. They did not have a budget. There was no retirement plan, and most did not have health insurance. Some did not have car insurance, not because they did not believe in it or wanted to test the Lord's provision—they simply couldn't afford it. They had to trust the Lord to take care of their vehicle.

I began to hear the word *itinerate*. "I've got to go itinerate," they would say. The evangelical missionary would go on furlough while the new breed would "go itinerate." That meant he would make a trip to the United States to visit supporting churches and look for new supporting churches. Many would go through years of financial hardship before having enough support. Of course, some did not make it and had to return home, but those that endured would become warriors.

I began to notice that among those that quit, some had excellent financial support. At that time, as I was struggling to survive, I could not understand why these well-funded missionaries could not make it. I remember one in particular. He had a new Suburban and ten times the support that I had, and he could not make it. I would find myself fantasizing about having his support. I learned that sacrifice and suffering were part of missionary formation.

Trait 5: They made their own decisions on the field.
There was not a missions board or a missions task force making decisions for them. Being able to be lead by the Holy Spirit was a high value to them. They decided where to live, work, and evangelize and when to move on. This was a key reason for their success. One of the Achilles heels of evangelical missions was that too many things were being decided by missions boards. The new breed would make their share of mistakes, but they would learn as they went and correct themselves.

Trait 6: They lived with the people.
Of course, there was not a European community like that in China during Hudson Taylor's time, where most missionaries lived. When I say they lived with the people, I mean they socialized with them, ate with them, and became friends with them. Unlike many

evangelical missionaries in China, who would socialize only with fellow Europeans, the new breed became part of the people. As time would pass, many would have more friends among the nationals than from their home country. Some would immigrate and become citizens of the country where they were serving. Many never planned on returning home to live. They would finish out their days in their adopted country.

Trait 7: They raised up and equipped national workers.

No one had to tell them, "Now, don't dominate the nationals. You need to raise up the nationals." It was a natural process for them to do so. After all, they lived with, socialized with, hung out with, played with, and ate with nationals. Unlike the traditional missionaries who would send their children off to school, the children of the new breed would be raised on the field. Their playmates would not be other American kids but nationals. There wasn't any missions infrastructure for them to fall back on. There was not any type of support system. They had no language schools. They had to learn Spanish on their own. Many whom I met did not speak Spanish very well for that reason. Some had tried to attend evangelical language schools, but were turned away because of their Pentecostal affiliation.

In 1979, my wife studied Spanish at Kingsway Missionary Institute in McAllen, Texas. Missionaries founded the school because the evangelical schools wouldn't accept Pentecostals or Charismatics. I remember a veteran missionary commenting that the evangelical Spanish school in nearby Edinburgh, Texas, was better than the one in Kingsway. "But they won't accept us," he sighed. Many times, the new breed missionaries struggled and persisted and learned Spanish despite the obstacles. I don't recall any of them being angry because of the rejection shown by their evangelical brethren. It didn't seem to bother them at all. They never whined, "If we could only have gone to school, our Spanish would be better." No obstacle could stop them because they knew that God was with them. The passion that filled their hearts propelled them on.

Trait 8: They were not highly educated.

Most were high school graduates, but hardly any were college grads. Those who had a degree in theology were few and far between. Others had a year or two of =Bible school. They were working-class men and women. They were sons and daughters of laborers, factory workers, farmers, Louisiana fishermen, and oil field workers.

Trait 9: They preached the Gospel to the poor and working-class Mexicans.

Being from a working-class background, they felt comfortable ministering to the working class. Many were born into poor families and remembered the struggles their parents went through. They identified with the working-class poor. I think many of them lacked the confidence to minister to professional and wealthy Mexicans. Others would eventually begin to penetrate the more educated classes. Their endeavors would cause the Pentecostal movement to become the dominant church group in Mexico.

I think their lack of education was actually a plus. The uneducated and lightly educated Mexicans could look at them and say, "I can be a minister, too." The highly educated evangelical missionary seemed to be less effective in raising up national workers. It may have been the social/educational gap between them and the working-class nationals that hindered the more professional evangelical minister. It would have been more difficult for the uneducated Mexican to look at the educated evangelical missionary and say, "I can be a minister like him."

Examples of the New Breed

Some of the new breed whom I knew or knew about were Frank Waren, Lola and Jerry Witt, Sister Allie, Danny Ost, and Bret Heart. They had a simple style that would also be easy to copy. Their preaching was highly exhortational and somewhat emotional—the perfect combination for reaching the multitudes of poor in Mexico.

As I mentioned, most of them were from small churches, and the churches they planted would, for the most part, remain small.

They modeled their new churches after their home churches where anyone could testify, share the Scriptures, or sing a special song. A typical church service in these Mexican churches would look like the following: After about an hour of worship and a time of sharing testimonies and Bible verses, people would sing special songs. Most had no singing ability, and some could not carry a tune in a bucket, but they always got "amen's." This could go on for an hour or more. More preaching would follow this, which could go on for forty-five minutes to an hour. This format made the typical church service a three-hour event.

I knew of one such church that grew to about two hundred members. Since they didn't change the way church was done, the services began to go four or five hours. The testimony time grew from an hour to two hours or more. After a while, the church began to decline. I knew of one woman whose husband wouldn't let her attend anymore for that very reason: He got tired of going to bed without his dinner.

The Second Wave

There was a lot of overlap between the new breed and the second wave. However, the difference was noticeable. The mainline Pentecostal movement was almost the sole producer of the new breed, but the Pentecostals, Charismatics, Evangelicals, and the Jesus movement would influence the second wave. They would build upon the foundation laid by the new breed. Most were influenced by, worked with, or knew new breed missionaries. You could not always tell them apart except by age.

The second wave exhibited most of the traits of the first wave or new breed. However, there were some key differences. For example, I think they took trait 6, living with the people, to a new level. Many became even more a part of the culture than their predecessors. Their history is still being written, so I can't say for certain, but I believe many will never return to live in their homeland.

Another difference was that the second wave were more educated. The second wavers would also speak better Spanish than the new breed. Their grammar was better, and their accent less prevalent. Of course, by then there were more language schools available as well as other helps for learning Spanish.

The second wave would also conduct their churches differently. They didn't use the new breed church model. Their preaching would be different as well. There would be more of a teaching flavor in their preaching. The second wave also brought new worship songs into the mix. The quality of music and worship began to improve. The older new breed missionaries would embrace the contemporary music introduced by the second wavers.

In Mexico, the second wave missionary would do something the new breed never accomplished on a large scale: They began to reach the more educated Mexicans. The second wavers discovered that the professional class non-Christians enjoyed socializing with them, so they used it for the Gospel and began to penetrate the wealthier and more educated class of Mexicans. Suddenly the churches now had a core of new believers who weren't poor. One of the first groups to be evangelized was schoolteachers. Most of them came from working class or poor backgrounds, so they were easy to reach, but soon the second wavers began to see doctors, lawyers, and business people receive Christ as well.

The second wave missionaries were also innovators. They found new ways to reach people. One example was when the VCR first came on the market. (Some of you must reveal your age, and admit that you remember!) For most of us, it is hard to remember a world without VCRs. Travel back in time with me to the birth of the VCR. There are no Blockbuster movie rentals. Now go with me to Mexico. There are no video movie rentals anywhere in Mexico. At that time, Mexico had a closed border. You weren't permitted to bring U.S. products into the country. Now with NAFTA, you just stop at a customs booth, pay taxes on what you want to import, and you go on your way. Back then, there wasn't anywhere to buy a VCR in Mexico, and VCRs were also expensive—about a thousand dollars or more. Add on inflation, and you get an idea of the cost.

A missionary took a VCR to Mexico along with some preaching tapes and discovered that everybody wanted to see this new marvel. We were all so amazed that this small box (or big box, by today's standards) could instantly produce a clear image on our TV. Missionaries soon discovered that the middle class and wealthy wanted to see this new scientific advance. No one seemed to mind watching a preacher. They were so enthralled with the devices that they didn't realize they were being evangelized. Suddenly, anyone who could come up with a thousand dollars for a VCR could have an effective evangelistic ministry. Many middle-class Mexicans were converted as a result of this ministry.

I still remember the day Alvin Lee called me and explained this phenomenon that was taking place. Alvin was a "helps missionary" whom I had met a few years before. "Do you have a VCR?" he asked. "No," I replied, "I don't have a thousand bucks lying around." "I'll see if I can get you one," Alvin replied. True to his word, a short time later he gave me a VCR with a stack of Praise the Lord Club videos in Spanish. This is a good example of people on the field being able to make fast decisions. This window of opportunity wouldn't be open for very long, but many missionaries took full advantage of it. Under the old system, by the time the mission board would have approved this plan, it would have been too late. They may have said, "Let's wait until the price of VCRs come down, and then we'll send you one." The new missionary sensed the briefness of the opportunity and seized the moment.

The New Breed Helps Missionary

Alvin Lee

About the time the second wavers were arriving, another group burst onto the mission scene: the helps missionaries. This new group, for the most part, would be in the age bracket of the new breed. Some were empty nesters, while others still had teenagers at home. They were hardworking men and women whose hearts had been captured for missions. Many wanted to learn Spanish, but despite their whole-hearted attempt, few were able to. They were at the age (late forties or fifties) that made it extremely difficult to learn a new language.

Alvin Lee was one of these helps missionaries who had moved to McAllen, Texas, from Oregon to study Spanish at Kingsway Missionary School. Alvin, along with his wife Margaret, endured nine months of torture at language school. We used to joke that people who learned a little Spanish knew just enough to get into trouble. After nine months of intensive study, Alvin didn't know enough Spanish to get into trouble. Most people would have packed it in and gone home, but not Alvin. He would almost single-handedly invent the modern helps ministry. He began to meet with missionaries and figure out ways to help them out. He heard I wanted to build a clinic in Fresnillo in central Mexico and brought a team of volunteers in his airplane. Alvin purchased a home in Alamo, Texas, near the Mexican border. He soon added on apartments for housing missionaries who needed a place to stay on their trips to the border.

In those days, missionaries would enter Mexico on tourist visas. The maximum amount of time allowed was one hundred eighty days. If the customs agents suspected that you were a missionary, they would give you less time. On one occasion, the customs agent asked me how much time I wanted, and I replied, "Six months." "Why do you want six months?" he questioned. He ended up giving me a thirty-day visa. So every six months or less, the missionaries had to make a trip to the border to get a new tourist visa. Word spread like wildfire about Alvin's open door. Nearly every missionary in Mexico sooner or later showed up at Alvin's house. It became a second home for many.

I can remember going to the border to get a new tourist visa and having only enough money to cover the gasoline. We didn't have any money for a hotel or to eat in restaurants. No problem—we went to Alvin's house. Alvin and Margaret never asked for money. I can remember many times when there where anywhere from six to twelve missionaries spending the night at Alvin's. It didn't matter how many. Margaret would call out, "Breakfast is ready." The dining room would fill up with missionaries for Margaret's biscuits and gravy. She was as incredible as her husband. Countless times I observed her joyfully preparing breakfast for whatever number of people that had arrived the night before. I never saw her do it unhappily or as though is was a burden. She was always joyful as she served God's missionaries.

Before Alvin was there to help out the poor missionaries, I remember on one occasion when we arrived at McAllen, Texas, from central Mexico that we had no money for hotels in those days, so we spent the night in the back of our pickup in August. It wasn't a pleasant night, but we survived. In the early years I don't know how we would have made it without Alvin and Margaret Lee being there. Alvin worked in more than a dozen countries over the years. He has left his mark everywhere. He built churches, Bible schools, orphanages, and feeding centers. Alvin constantly recruited people to go on mission trips. When he found someone like himself with leadership skills and building skills, he would bring that person alongside for a while and then encourage his new student to launch out on his or her own. Who knows how many new ministries were born because they came into contact with Alvin Lee.

After several years of ministering at the border, Alvin moved to Oklahoma, where he continued his aggressive mission work. By then, most missionaries were doing better financially, and a couple other missionary assistance ministries had set up shop along the border. We used to joke about the poor guy who bought Alvin's house. Who knows how many missionaries walked into his house while he was watching TV! There were probably some that knocked on his door at 1:00 a.m. We always thought about driving by to see if he had a big sign stating "Alvin doesn't live here anymore."

Malcolm and Hazel Hancock

Other amazing new breed helps missionaries were Malcolm and Hazel Hancock. Malcolm was so much like Alvin that I would often call Alvin "Malcolm" or call Malcolm "Alvin." Malcolm and Hazel live in Victoria, Texas. Malcolm also had an open door for any missionary who needed lodging. It didn't matter what your church affiliation was—you were welcome at Malcolm's. It didn't matter what time you arrived, or if you were expected or not. If you arrived in the middle of a meal, they wouldn't ask if you were hungry; they would already be in motion, putting more plates on the table. "Set down and eat," they would say. You always felt more than welcome at Malcolm's. He was one of those incredible men of God who wanted only to serve you. He would do anything. He would cook, do construction or labor of any kind. Malcolm has helped me load countless trucks destined for Mexico with used clothes, heavy medical equipment, food, medicines, and many other things.

For a period of a few years, I was smuggling Bibles and New Testaments into Mexico. For some reason, Mexican customs blocked the import of Bibles for a while, so I began smuggling them into Mexico. I can remember calling Malcolm and saying, "I've got a semitrailer of Bibles coming in. I'm by myself and need help unloading them." He would get some people together and be there. I stopped by to visit him in August 2002 and asked him how many Bibles we smuggled in to Mexico. He put the number at 250,000.

For the twenty-four years I have known Malcolm, I have never seen him get angry, upset, or impatient. I can remember trying to get through customs at the Mexican border with a school bus full of things that the customs agents said we couldn't take into the country. We waited seven or eight hours in the hot sun as we tried to convince the authorities to let us in. During that time, Malcolm never became angry or impatient while I paced back and forth and was frustrated by our lack of progress.

The church that Malcolm attended had a great deal of passion for missions. People were encouraged to be involved and to financially support missionaries and missions. One time, we were heading to Illinois for a visit and stopped at Malcolm's to spend the night. It was a service night, so we attended church with him. They gave us the traditional greeting from the pulpit, announcing that Brother Fred, a missionary from Mexico, was visiting. I was completely surprised with what happened when the service was dismissed. Many people, after shaking my hand, put money or checks into my shirt pocket. I was amazed. No one told them to do it. The pastors and elders were full of passion for missions, and they taught their people to be passionate about missions. If my memory is correct, more that two hundred dollars were stuffed into my pocket. It was a fair amount considering no offering was taken and the church wasn't very large. I had witnessed and experienced first-hand the Charismatic zeal for missions.

I regard it as an honor having known men and women like Alvin and Margaret Lee, and Malcolm and Hazel Hancock. They were true soldiers and some of God's best saints. One of my concerns is our modern pastors' lack of knowledge of these missionaries. It seems they are all still looking at the failures of the colonial and evangelical missionaries and saying, "We're not going to repeat their mistakes." We need to learn from the new breed. Instead of worrying so much about repeating the failures of evangelical missions, we need to build upon the success of the new breed and second wavers. We need to contextualize their model for the twenty-first century.

They Weren't All Keepers

I hope I haven't given the impression that all who left for the mission field were cutting-edge, highly effective missionaries. There were some who, even though they came from a Pentecostal background and were faith based, would continue in some colonial practices. They had that Pentecostal passion for missions, but because of lack of knowledge, they mixed in some colonial missions practices. The most common colonial tradition they practiced was paying the salaries of national workers and pastors. In the long run, they would not be as effective as the less colonial new breeds.

This group came to my attention again recently when a young man, whose church had joined our church movement, wanted to talk with me about the mission work that he was doing. He was working with a missionary who was in bad health and trying to hand most of the work over to him. The older missionary had built ten churches over the years in small villages in northern Mexico. From what I understood, since the older man had not been spending much time in Mexico anymore because of health issues, most or all of the churches had been locked up. The new man was given the keys to the churches and turned loose. He told me that he wanted to share with me what he was doing and correct him if he was doing anything wrong.

He was hiring men to pastor the small churches that he had inherited. Whenever he had a guest speaker from the United States, he felt obligated to fill up the church for the visiting preacher. However, the only way to accomplish that was to announce that, after the service, those attending would receive a free bag of groceries or other items. I had to restrain myself from saying, "You're doing everything wrong:" His methods were all wrong, but I liked everything else. He had passion for missions and a high level of commitment. I knew it was a matter of getting him pointed in the right direction. I saw more potential in him than in others who have studied all the methods but have an air of arrogance and an "I know how to do it" attitude. Someone with real zeal and passion for souls can be pointed in the right direction and become very effective. However, someone who fears being like a colonial missionary, even though his methods are better than the passionate person, will not always be successful.

There were a number of men and women whom I can only classify as characters. I came into contact with some of these characters at Kingsway Missionary Institute in McAllen, Texas where my wife studied Spanish. I borrowed a camper, which I parked at the school for my wife to stay in. She began to take classes, and I returned to Mexico. I got things in order so I could return to the school for a couple of months. Don, the director of the school, gave me permission to sit in on the classes at no charge. That was helpful because I was still working on my Spanish.

We were perpetually broke at that time, and we always did what we could to cut corners. It can get very hot in south Texas, but we seldom used the air conditioning because we just couldn't afford it. Joe, another student who had a big forty-foot camper parked a few stalls from us, was always on my case about my lack of faith to trust the Lord to supply the money for our electrical bill. I had already classified Joe as a character, so I never took his rebuke to heart. If it got too hot, I could always step in for a visit at Joe's. His air ran day and night, and his humungous trailer was always well chilled.

One night, I stopped by to see Joe. He was always fun to hang around with. When I stepped into his trailer, I notice that he had several candles lit. I was so used to the heat by then that I didn't notice that his air conditioning was turned off. I looked at the candles and, thinking that he had a romantic evening planned with his wife, excused myself for having interrupted his plans. Joe explained that it wasn't the case. "What's with the candles, Joe?" I inquired. "Well, today they shut off my electricity because I couldn't pay the bill." I didn't say a word. My carnal man had a few choice lines that I could have blurted out, but I decided not to. I think his humiliation was enough without me throwing a few more sticks on the fire.

One day I was praying and said, "God, how are we going to evangelize Mexico with so many characters?" About 25 percent of the school was made up of the character category. It was as though God spoke to me and said, "They are available, and people will hear the Gospel through them."

Evangelist Bob and the One-Hour Revival

Bob, a Charismatic evangelist, was another character. I often wondered why Bob even attended language school. He would do anything to distract the teachers. Remember, the school was run by people from Pentecostal and Charismatic backgrounds. A few of the teachers were easily sidetracked. Evangelist Bob and his little prophecy-focused group knew which ones were the pushovers, and they would always have a Bible question or a prophecy to give before class started. They were often successful at delaying the start of class.

The school also had a tradition. Once a year, all the male teachers would go deer hunting together. This was Texas, after all. Don, the founder of the school, was a no-nonsense Pentecostal who wouldn't tolerate any distractions in his classes. Well, the day came that the cat was away and the Charismatic mice began to play. At the 11:00 a.m. class, Bob and company began by prophesying. Then Bob declared that we needed to seek the Lord and everyone was to go to the chapel. The classroom emptied. Word spread to the other classes, and they also poured into the chapel. I was thinking, "Maybe Bob's right this time. The whole school is here praying." I recalled other revivals. I wondered if they would pray all night. I wouldn't have to wait a long for the answer. At noon the lunch bell rang, and as fast as the revival had started, it ended. Within seconds, evangelist Bob was out the door and on his way to the cafeteria. The revival was over. My friend Jack and I just stood there looking at one another, amazed that the lunch bell could so speedily end this mighty revival. I don't know what happened to evangelist Bob, and

I hope to keep it that way. I doubt if he ever made it to Mexico. Bob was a category 5 character—the kind you hope will never leave their house.

There were an assortment of characters, most of whom were in the lower or harmless category. I remember two young men in particular who were behind on their payment to the school. Easter break was coming up, and the school was going to have a long recess. Jack and I took advantage of the opportunity and found work with a local contractor. We both owed the school money and wanted to have it paid by the end of the school year. Our boss told us that he could use a couple more guys if we knew anyone looking for a few days' work. Jack and I both thought of the two young men who owed money. When I told them about the opportunity to make a few bucks toward paying their bill, they declined the offer, saying that they were trusting God to supply the money for their tuition. They were basically good guys with a bad hyperfaith doctrine.

One of the more wacky ones was a man who, after finishing school, planned to raise money for a yacht. When I asked what he would do with a yacht on the mission field, he explained that his plan was to install some huge speakers and sail around preaching to coastal villages from the comfort and security of his yacht. I did not follow his career, but I am sure that donations rolled in. Who wouldn't want to support a yacht ministry? If you shop around, you can find a good yacht for under a half million dollars!

Bread Truck Bob

I met another Bob on one of my first trips to Mexico. I was in a service at a church in Monterrey where Bob was teaching. I believe he was in his sixties at that time (in the mid-1970s). Bob was a clean-cut, well-kept man who had a bread truck that he had made into a camper. One of the first things I remember about him was his comment after church: "I need to go." He meant that he needed to go wash his hands. He wasn't used to shaking hands with so many poor people.

Bob was a little weird. The young Mexican guys whom I was running with at the time used to make jokes about Bob and his bread truck. One day I was with Bob in his camper and asked him where his spare tire was. "I don't carry one," he said, "that's just asking for trouble. I trust God to take care of my tires." Somehow he equated having a spare tire to lack of faith and that it would cause him to have a flat tire.

A few months later, I was with Bob again. He was looking for something under the seat and pulled out a big handgun. "What is that?" I asked in astonishment. "I would never travel in Mexico without packing iron," he said. Now, maybe it is just me, but I could never figure out how deliberately not carrying a spare tire was a sign of faith and packing a forty-five was not a sign of lack of faith. I didn't know it at the time, but if a person was caught carrying a gun in Mexico, it was an automatic prison sentence.

I never saw Bob again after that. It may have been because he got caught and was in prison, I don't know.

As weird as Bread Truck Bob was, let's give him credit. While other men were in retirement watching television all day, he was going for it. He had guts and that Pentecostal passion for missions. Imagine a guy his age packing up and going to Mexico. My hat is off to Bob—or, should I say, I raise my pistol in his memory.

CHAPTER 4

Colonial Missionary Complex

Some pastors, ministries, missions agencies, missions groups, task forces, and para-church groups suffer from what I call "Colonial Missionary Complex," or CMC. They carry the burden of the mistakes of the colonial missionary. They have studied the evangelical missions agency missionary and seen their shortcomings, and the negative way many of them treated the nationals in whatever country they worked. They have determined to correct the attitude and behavior exhibited by the colonial missionary. They want to avoid any resemblance to the colonial missionary and they fear repeating their mistakes.

What Were Some of the Mistakes of the Colonial Missionaries?
It started with their cultural worldview. At that time (the 1800s–1900s), Western culture was seen as superior to the more pagan-dominated cultures of the other nations. After all, they reasoned, weren't they more advanced industrially and politically with their growing democracies? Wasn't Christianity the only true religion and therefore superior to the paganism of other nations? Wasn't Western society superior?

Examples of practices in Eastern cultures seemed to give proof to this idea. In India, when a husband died, the wife was burned to death at the funeral. In China, girls' feet were bound in order to stunt their growth. In some parts of Africa, girls were circumcised and sold as wives. The list could go on. The prevailing secular attitude at the time was that Western culture was obviously superior. The Christian church adopted the secular attitude of the times.

How Did These Attitudes Play Out in the Form of Practices?

Our general view of the colonial missionaries, as we look back and study them (sometimes judgmentally), is that they dominated the nationals. They didn't trust the nationals enough to turn the work and authority over to them. The missionaries really didn't think the nationals were capable of running things. At the time, the standard practice was for the missionary to pay the salary of the national worker or pastor, and therefore, the power rested with the missionary. The one who pays the salary is the boss. To keep your job (salary), you need to do things as the boss wants. The missionary and the national could never be equals for one was the employer and the other the employee. Both the cultural view and the foreign money kept the missionary from being able to deal with the nationals as equals. The colonial missionaries also had difficulty raising up self-supporting churches. Making the nationals dependent on outside money largely contributed to this problem.

To sum it up, the colonial missionary ran the show. He controlled things. He made the decisions, did the planning, and told the nationals where to work. There wasn't any partnership. There was no equality. There wasn't a team. The nationals weren't encouraged to have vision. The colonial missionaries would decide that. In some cases, the foreign missionary or agency owned the church properties

The new Reformed Evangelical missionaries are often overly conscious of the shortcomings of their predecessors and very determined to do things differently. They are paranoid about dominating the nationals or even the appearance of domination.

Mission boards, leaders, and task forces are experiencing the same thing. They feel compelled to correct the dysfunctional ways of the colonial missionary. Therefore, they will develop a new list of rules and regulations to ensure that the missionary will never go down that road again. If colonial tendencies surface, the list will keep missionaries under control.

What contributes to this paranoia that causes missions leaders to come up with these rules? I call it Colonial Missionary Complex (CMC). Around 1997, I began to notice the symptoms of this problem, though I had not discovered the root cause or named the illness. It began to come to my attention when a missionary shared about his denomination. The denomination hadn't been very active in missions in the past, and they decided that it was time to get involved. Their missions leaders visited him on the field and explained their new policy for missions. The missions leader stated that a missionary could only have authority as pastor in one local church. In other words, he couldn't be an overseer of anything more than the one local church where he was pastor. He could never function as overseer of any new church plants or any group of churches. It didn't matter whether or not he was directly involved in the planting of new churches. At the time, the missionary couldn't figure out the logic or the motive for this thinking. He felt that it was not only unbiblical and impractical but also a foolish policy formulated by people who didn't speak a second language or had never worked in a foreign country as missionaries. The best way to raise up leaders is to model for them and thereby train them how to lead.

This denomination had several other new policies as they attempted to do missions in a new and different way. It wasn't until later that my missionary friend figured out that his denominational leaders' assumption was that he was a colonial-type missionary. They assumed that he was exercising too much authority over the nationals. He was judged to be a classic colonial missionary, and the new missions thinkers were going to keep him in check and protect the nationals from his domination. After all, these new mission thinkers had studied the colonial missionary and found him wanting. They had read books on missions and now they felt they were knowledgeable enough to do things the right way. It didn't matter that they had never been missionaries or planted churches in another culture. They knew what the errors of the colonial missionaries were, and they would correct them.

I call this "Reactionary Missions Strategy." Most of this policy is an overreaction to something that was done wrong in the past. Their thinking is dominated by CMC. They need to reaffirm to the nationals that they are not there to be their boss or to tell them how to do things. "You tell us how you want us to help you," they tell the nationals. These statements help the CMC sufferer reaffirm that he is not acting like the classic "colonial" missionary.

The more severe cases of CMC can even become antimissionary. Some church movements and denominations have missions departments that are suffering from "Severe Colonial Missionary Complex" (SCMC). Their strategy does not emphasize the importance of sending missionaries. Some see the missionary as a hindrance or an obstacle to their missions work. They think it best to work directly with the nationals. They don't want or need a missionary. They don't see the missionary as a bridge between the cultures. This philosophy can and does present some problems and dangers.

This is especially true for denominations that want to start church planting movements in another country. If you don't send missionaries to plant the first churches and get it going, then how do you do it? You can't plant a church by making a one-week missions trip to another country. If you don't send men and women to plant the first churches that will grow into a church-planting movement, then what are your options? You have to find existing churches that want to join your denomination, or you have to recruit Christian leaders from existing churches that are willing to plant churches for you. You put your denominational name on the church plant and claim you are planting a church overseas. You might get away with doing missions this way in larger cities of the highly evangelized countries. It may be a long time before you are even noticed. However, in the under evangelized countries and cities, you tend to stand out more. You are in danger of the nationals seeing you as someone looking to put your name on someone else's work or as someone not willing to make converts, then disciple them and raise them up as leaders. You have come to "grab" leaders who were converted and developed by someone else.

In 1995, we moved to the west coast of Mexico to plant a church. The local pastors were very suspicious of us because a U.S. church from our denomination had been making annual trips there, ministering in many of their churches. Because of this, they feared that we would use the relationships that this church had developed to pull people out of their churches to start our own. I met with the Mexican pastors and explained that we had no intention of planting a church by recruiting their members. They embraced us with some reservations and told us that anyone willing to evangelize and plant churches was welcome in Mexico. As time went on, they saw that we were true to our word and didn't build a church with their converts. In fact, their suspicion then turned into respect. I am sure that the national pastors in other countries would react in a similar fashion if treated with similar care and sensitivity.

The Dangers of Burning Bridges

Severe CMC antimissionary people also place themselves in danger by removing the bridge between two cultures. The antimissionary CMC sufferers are prone to make many mistakes. Like their predecessor the colonial missionary, their mistakes may not be revealed for years. By eliminating the missionary, who serves as a source of vital information to help them avoid doing dumb things, they remove the bridge between the two cultures. I am assuming of course, that you have a new breed missionary to work with. If you happen to be working through a classic colonial missionary, then this point doesn't matter.

I have heard of many mistakes being made as a result of working without cultural bridges. One of the more common mistakes is building churches on land assumed to be church property and finding out later that it wasn't the case. In one instance, a pastor from the United States wanted to help the church that they were ministering to in Latin America to become self-sufficient. So they set the church up with a small business including an addition to the church from which the small business would operate. Some time after the pastor and his team returned to the United States, a church split occurred as a result of the business. It turned out that the building where the church was meeting belonged to the pastor. A good number of people left, so he shut down the church and kept the business going. Having a knowledgeable missionary involved could have avoided the whole problem. A missions group, wanting to do good, instead harmed the national Christians.

CMC has the potential to harm and hinder modern missions. It tends to cause people to do things in a mechanical way and very often in extremes. True humility of heart and a profound love for people eliminate the need for most arbitrary and petty rules.

How Does One Get This Terrible Illness?

CMC is normally acquired by focusing too much on the dysfunctional colonial missionary and reading books that center on the same. Then how do we avoid contracting CMC? The answer is not to study only the failures while attempting to successfully correct their shortcomings. The best plan is to study the successful missionaries, learn the things that they did right, and build on these successes.

Peter Drucker, the well-known management guru and consultant, said something that illustrates the point I am trying to make. He said something to the effect of, "When managing or developing people, we can only build on strengths, not weaknesses. When we truly build on strengths, weaknesses become irrelevant." This is the principle I am talking about. We should build upon the strengths of successful new breed missionaries in place of concentrating too much on the weaknesses of the colonial missionary. Study those who I call the new breed—men like Anthony Groves, Hudson Taylor, C. T. Studd, J. O. Fraiser, and the modern day new breeds of the 1950s through and 1970s.

The Ugly Gringo

We have all heard about the classic book *The Ugly American*. The missions department of one church headquarters has it on the list of recommended reading for missions. Some of the other books are Roland Allen's books, as well as a few "Where did we go wrong?" style books. For some time now, I have been concerned more with what is *not* on the list. Since the list of books to read is composed mostly of books on methods or how we messed up, I believe it to be an unhealthy balance that could contribute to Colonial Missionary Complex. The list lacks material that can spark passion and inspiration. A few well-chosen missionary biography books would bring a healthy balance. Passion needs to be a driving force if we are to be effective in missions. Please note that I didn't say that we need to be fanatical, extreme, or "loco." Passion is what moved Hudson Taylor to break from the more colonial-type missions societies and move in a different direction.

The Ugly American is a blistering critique of American foreign policy during the Cold War era. I was surprised to find a lot of things in the book that go along with advice that I have been giving on missions. The authors, William Lederer and Eugene Burdick, show how American foreign policy was losing the battle for the minds of the people to the communists. In the book, none of the ambassadors or key people speak the language of the country to which they are assigned, nor do they understand the customs or the culture. In no way did the Americans try to blend in. On the other hand, the Soviet counterpart studied the language, the customs, and the culture of the people that they would be working with; the result was that the Soviets were much more successful in winning people over than the Americans were. The authors also portray several men as the "good" or "successful" Americans. These fictional good guys remind me of the new breed missionaries. They were passionate, lived with the people, respected the culture, were somewhat independent, and didn't want too much central control over their activities. These good guys were portrayed as grassroots-type people.

The book is fictional but is based on events that actually took place. Most of the dumb characters in the book didn't realize that they were dumb. The new generation of dumb gringos probably couldn't see themselves in the book. *The Ugly American* concludes by recommending that all future ambassadors be required to study the language of his or her assigned country. The root cause of our failures overseas begins with the people in charge not being able to speak the language.

I find it ironic that some of the same missions people who recommend this book are violating its most important principles. The particular group that recommends *The Ugly American* is determined to do missions in a new way and has skipped the part about learning the language of the country you are assigned to. Their international coordinator, who recommended the book, doesn't even speak a foreign language. The Latin American missions coordinator also does not speak a second language. You would think it would be a no-brainer that if you were in charge of missions in a large portion of the world where they all spoke the same language, maybe you should dedicate an hour a day toward learning that language. Could it be that even though they are determined to do missions the right way, they are repeating the mistakes of the past? Is it also possible that they will not see their dumbness until years later when someone writes about it? One of the major mistakes of colonial missions was that men who didn't speak the language, and who didn't live in the country or thoroughly understand the culture with which the missionaries were working, were the same men formulating policies for missions. The dumb gringo is alive and well and repeating the mistakes of the past because he is telling himself that he will do missions in a new way without being colonial.

The principles that the authors of *The Ugly American* gave to correct our diplomatic problems can also be applied to missions. They recognized the errors of the ambassadors and embassy personnel. Then, they looked at the few Americans who were doing it right and said we should follow their example. I believe we can approach missions in the same way. Let's take a look at the failures of the colonial missionary and then direct our attention to the successful missionaries in order to build on their success.

The Roland Allen Model

Many evangelicals look to Roland Allen to form their missions policy. He is, for many, the high priest of missions strategy. However, in my opinion, Allen's books are one of the sources causing CMC. There is a very definite danger if anyone depends too much on Roland Allen for developing his or her mission philosophy. I have read both of Allen's books, *The Spontaneous Expansion of the Church* and *Missionary Methods*, at least twice and have found them to be helpful.

I continue to recommend and give copies of Allen's books to certain people, but not to everyone. I believe that some will read Allen's books and become convinced that because they read the books, they know how to do missions. Others will develop Colonial Missionary Complex and become overly paranoid in the way they relate to nationals. Such people have the potential to make many mistakes on the mission field without realizing that they are doing so until long after the damage is done. If you are upset by my critique of Allen, you might be one of these people.

I think most people have neglected to heed some of the warnings that are written in the two forewords of Allen's book *The Spontaneous Expansion of the Church*. For example, in one foreword, the following is stated:

> On the other hand I have heard of mission boards which decided to "apply" Allen's methods, and proceeded to issue instructions to "the field" accordingly. The result could only be disaster. There are no "methods" here that will "work" if they are "applied." There is a summons to everyone who will hear to submit inherited patterns of the Church life to the searching scrutiny of the Spirit. (Bishop Lesslie Newbigin)

Newbigin also asserts, "Allen was a missionary of the Society of the Propagation of the Gospel. He was a priest of the church of England nurtured in the Catholic understanding of churchmanship."

In the second foreword, Kenneth G. Grubb makes this observation and gives a word of warning:

> At the same time, it is important to remember that Allen, no less than any other author, must be read with discrimination and judgment, and in some passages with reservations. They are not skillful framers of policies who swallow any man's views wholesale and give them what might be termed an almost mechanical interpretation, in a world where issues—spiritual, political, moral and economic—are intertwined with the utmost delicacy and complexity.

He also says, "By common and willing consent the era of missionary domination in the Church has gone and it is no longer possible for the missionary to dominate the Church; it has always been undesirable. Even at the time of this writing, the era of missionary domination of the foreign churches had, for the most part, already passed."

One problem is that when people read Roland Allen, they get the idea that missionary domination is still a major problem on the mission field when, in fact, it is not. The Roland Allen type of dysfunctional missionary has passed. So one danger of his books is that people read them and assume that all of these problems still exist. They therefore overreact to these phantom problems because they are predisposed toward that type of judgment after depending too much on Allen for developing their mission strategy.

Certain people, however, can benefit from Roland Allen. Some missionaries have a tendency to stay too long in one place instead of handing the work over to the nationals. I like to give the Allen book to such people. A few years back, I sent a copy to the head of a missions group because I had seen that they were staying too long and not handing the work over to the nationals. I would not recommend the book to somebody just beginning mission work because I believe they would make the same mistakes that many have made, overreacting and being too paranoid about dominating nationals.

Some people read books on missions and even though they have never planted a church in another country, they act as if they were experts. One thing that some people do not keep in mind is that it is not the same world as it was in Allen's time. People are not that much in awe of the West anymore. For example, in my church in Mazatlán, we have two members, an engineer who runs a huge thermoelectric plant and an owner of a hotel in the tourist "Golden Zone," who are somewhat anti-American. They are not in awe of Americans or the West whatsoever. If I were to try to dominate them, I wouldn't last very long. They accept my leadership because I come in as their equal, live with them, and fellowship with them. As Grubb notes in the foreword of *The Spontaneous Expansion of the Church*, the time when the missionaries could dominate the church has passed. You couldn't make it happen now if you tried, because the majority of the cultures in this world would no longer accept it. Mission societies have come a long way since then. Very few remain that are as dysfunctional as Allen's was.

Jim Egli, a good friend of mine, is a fine example of what can happen if you depend too much on Allen. Jim was a missionary in

Africa some years ago. He relied heavily on Roland Allen for his missionary strategy. Jim commented that in Africa you could always spot the Roland Allen missionaries (that is, those who's missionary thinking had been formed by Allen's writing) because they all put African names on their Bible schools, whereas none of the Bible schools started by Africans had African names. All their schools had English names. That conversation with Jim prompted me to ask him to write a paper on missions. The following is an excerpt from that paper:

Vineyard Mission in the 21st Century
Reflections of a Missions Advocate

In the fall of 2001, I had some extended time with the author when I was in Mexico to do some training for Mexican leaders on relational evangelism and small-group ministry. During our time together I was discussing the mistakes that I had made as a missionary in Africa in the 1980s and what I see as critical for the future of Vineyard missions. I was asked to jot down my thoughts. I have an ongoing concern for cross-cultural ministry. I have lived in Africa, Europe, and Central America and have written discipleship training materials that have been translated into diverse languages including Spanish, Russian, Portuguese and Korean. More recently my thinking has been sharpened as I have completed a Ph.D. in communication from Regent University that included a minor in world evangelization.

A Global Village
It was a sunny winter day in Umtata, Transkei, South Africa, where I was leading a Bible training conference for Xhosa pastors and church leaders. I had just finished lunch and was relaxing at the table when a group of the pastors approached me to raise an important issue.

Several months before, we had launched a new leadership training program and response had exceeded our expectations. Soon about 40 African leaders would complete our first round of training conferences covering the four Gospels, and we would award them a certificate to celebrate and recognize their accomplishment.

The leaders who approached me said, "Pastor Jim, we need a name for our Bible training program." I wholeheartedly agreed. The conversation that followed, however, was very convoluted, and it was only later that I realized how much I had to learn about cross-cultural ministry. The Xhosa leaders preferred a name such as "Transkei Bible Institute." I knew, however, how inappropriate that would be. Why pick an English name when the program was for the Xhosa? I recommended they select a Xhosa name. I told them how a similar program in neighboring Lesotho was called "Alosa Linku Tsa Ka," or feed my sheep, a Sesotho name with a motif that was both biblical and culturally relevant to southern Africa.

The best way I can describe the ensuing discussion was grid-lock. The Africans showed no interest in embracing a Xhosa name, and I had no interest in their English suggestions. No name was chosen then, or in the months ahead. It was only much later that I realized what had really happened that beautiful afternoon in Umtata.

My understanding of that encounter and its implications began later when I noticed that all leadership training programs with African names were actually named by whites and that the Africans consistently gave their training programs English names! It was somewhat unsettling to realize that missionaries like me were, in fact, gently forcing African names on African programs, names that the Africans themselves would only choose under our well-intended but misguided coercion.

It was a strange new imperialism! Nineteenth-century missionaries had imposed European styles of dress and worship on Africans, and now a century later when the Africans wanted to choose English names for their programs, some of us were cramming African names on them.

On further reflection, I realized that most new African churches and denominations had English names rather than African names. All the Africans where I lived know some English. English has so penetrated their culture that everyone used English numbers. (It's easier to say "twenty-two" than to say "mashome a mabedi le metse a medi"!) They wanted to use English names because all accredited schools had English names. Having an English name communicated credibility and permanence.

My mission logical assumptions had been shaped by Roland Allen—a strategic missions thinker that I continue to admire. But I was discovering that both the questions and answers were shifting in our changing world.

Jim Egli

I believe that Jim developed a mild case of colonial missionary complex as a result of relying too much on Roland Allen. He was overly conscious of something looking colonial or acting like a colonial missionary. It is ironic that, while consciously trying not to be a colonial missionary, he, for a short time, behaved like one. To his credit, he figured out his mistake and was secure enough to share his story with me. I can picture a modern missions board, feeling quite capable of making wise decisions because they have read all the books, saying, "Now, what would be a good African name for our Bible schools?"

Of all the changes that Hudson Taylor made in missions, I believe that this one is the least implemented and the most difficult to accept. I think it will be very difficult for someone who has studied missions and read "all the books" to understand and accept that they are still not the most qualified to run missions. To give up power is something that is extremely difficult to do. What do those who are qualified to run missions look like? Having lived in a foreign land or having served as a missionary for many years does not automatically qualify you.

Roland Allen was a missionary with the Church of England. The missions program he worked with was very dysfunctional and the missionaries very colonial. Out of his experience with a dysfunctional missions society, Allen wrote the two books I mentioned, in which he critiqued his church's missionaries and gave his view on how missions should be done. Allen was a brilliant man, very intelligent, and light-years ahead of his time in his views. In his books, he has some helpful things to say on missions.

Without a doubt, these books had to be written. Colonial missions needed to be challenged. A strong prophetic rebuke was in order. The trumpet had to be sounded, and Roland Allen sounded it. Some were offended, others rejected his critique, and some tried to apply Allen's methods without success. The books did make many missionaries and missions agencies examine themselves.

However, his books have a couple of major flaws that I don't think have been exposed and critiqued. First, his book on missionary methods is predicated on the idea that the Apostle Paul had no particular advantage over modern missionaries, and therefore he is the standard for success by which we measure ourselves. The second flaw is that Allen believed that because the methods that he espoused are all derived from the Bible (mostly from the Book of Acts), his book would never be out of date. When his readers buy into that, they close the door to other options. I have already refuted those two things in my chapter "Compelling Factors and the Book of Acts."

Bruce L. Shelley, the respected church historian and author of *Church History in Plain Language*, mentions the group labeled "God-Fearers" when comparing evangelism today with first-century results. Remember, the God-Fearers were gentiles who had accepted the God of Israel and the Scriptures but did not want to go through the circumcision ritual. They were not allowed to enter the synagogue, so they would gather outside to listen. Every synagogue had a group of God-Fearers. When they heard the Gospel, they learned that they could have a relationship with God without circumcision, and they responded in large numbers. This easy-to-reach group with its high standard of morality would accelerate Paul's church-planting ability. If this one factor were taken out of the equation, Paul's results would not have been the same. Shelley says that this one group makes it impossible to make comparisons. He writes:

> The presence of this prepared elite [the God-Fearers] makes comparisons of evangelism in the age of the apostles and any later age almost impossible. Most of the "God-fearers" knew the Old Testament well; they understood its theological ideas; they accepted its moral values. Few, if any other missionary move-

ments in Christian history could look upon such a prepared field for harvesting.

When Paul started in Ephesus, Priscilla and Aquila had already been there for a good while planting the church. Paul also had another blessing that would accelerate the maturity of the new church in Ephesus, the conversion of twelve men who were committed followers of John the Baptist (Acts 19:1). After that, he went to the synagogue to harvest Jews, Proselytes, and the God-fearers. We can conclude that Paul had several things in his favor when he started in Ephesus. He had Priscilla and Aquila along with their converts. Apollos helped out for a while. Twelve dedicated followers of John the Baptist were converted, as well as Jews and God-Fearers.

Anyone who says that Paul had no particular advantage has never planted a church in an unevangelized area where you're starting from ground zero. I have, and I can tell you it takes a lot of work and perseverance to get twelve dedicated men raised up. As I have already stated, if Paul were to return today and preach in the same cities and countries that are now Muslim dominated, I don't think he would measure up to the first-century Paul.

There are other factors in Allen's teaching that should be mentioned. One weakness is that there was no vision for lay missionaries. Being an Anglican missionary himself probably blinded him to that possibility. Another thing that Allen stated, which I think is close to being ridiculous, was that he believed the great commission didn't apply to us today as it did to the Apostles. One only has to look at the Pentecostal movement to see the folly of that statement. "Go ye into all the world" was the banner of the early Pentecostals. Look at the fruit worldwide as a result of their applying the Matthew 28 text to themselves. Millions have been saved as a result of the Pentecostal missionary zeal.

These are some of the reasons why I have a huge problem relying on Roland Allen for developing a missions strategy. He never put his own theories and methods to the test. We don't know how many of his methods and theories actually work, because they were never tested on the mission field by Allen. The fact that Allen wrote with such authority and because his writing was very compelling, many people swallow his advice hook, line, and sinker. I find it disturbing that so many people make Allen their major source for missions thinking.

To sum it up, Allen's ideas were exactly what was needed for those under the influence of modernism and colonialism. However, when Westerners who are influenced by post modern thought read Allen, the results can be disastrous. They are in danger of contracting CMC.

Looking at it from another angle, let's say you want to start a business making and marketing Article X. You hear about John Doe who tried to start the same business but whose company failed. John Doe has written a book on how to start a company that makes and sells Article X. In his book he tells you what he did wrong and then presents his theories on how to successfully start a business. Would you be so foolish as to rely on a man who never successfully started a business as your main source of guidance? Or would you buy Jane Doe's book on how to start a business, knowing that she started one from the ground up, making and marketing Article X, and that her company was the most successful in its field? Which of the two would you make as your main source of information? I would hope the latter. After having thoroughly studied Jane Doe, you might consider reading John Doe as well.

What Conditions Can Help Incubate CMC?

I believe that some of the same conditions that helped produce the dysfunctional colonial missionary are present in modern evangelical missions. When the majority of those who make up our missions leaders and missionaries are seminary-trained people, I believe it creates the conditions that produce colonial missionaries as well as causing colonial missionary complex.

In 2001, a large number of Mazatlán pastors got together and invited a pastor from Argentina to come and hold a training conference. They asked if they could use our facility, to which I gladly agreed. One day I gave Rosendo, the guest pastor, a tour of our work in Mazatlán and shared our four-point strategy. He already had a good-size church, but he thought he could apply some of our strategy to his work. Some time later he was invited back by the Mazatlán pastors. He sought me out, and we met for breakfast. I told him I was stepping down and turning over our main church to a Mexican national. "I thank God for missionaries," he said. "I was led to the Lord by missionaries, but they weren't like you." His experience had been with traditional evangelical seminary trained missionaries. When he wanted to work in the ministry, he was told that he should go to seminary first. He went on to share how they didn't really trust the Argentineans or think that they could do a good job. "You're different," he told me. He went on to explain how he was impressed by the way I trusted the Mexicans and put them in charge of our colonia (neighborhood) churches and ministries. I felt honored by his endorsement.

When Will Mission Agencies Learn to Lower the Bar?

Have we learned nothing from history? When Hudson Taylor lowered the bar and accepted unordained and lightly educated men and women into the China Inland Mission, his mission became the most effective of its time. The Methodist revival in England began to expand at an incredible rate when John Wesley accepted lay preachers. When the Methodist Church in the 1800s in the United States had a lay-dominated ministry, they demonstrated great spiritual power and grew to be the largest denomination in the country. The same observations can be made of the early Pentecostal movement. The key person in the rapid expansion of Pentecostalism was William Symore, a lightly educated black man with poor personal hygiene. With strong lay leadership, it grew to become a dominant worldwide force.

I am not trying to create an inferiority complex in seminary-trained men and women, but facts are facts and history is history. Professional ministry is like the legal profession. We need some lawyers around, but too many in society can really screw things up. If you were called by God to seminary, then I am sure my comments won't bother you because you know you are numbered among those whom we need. I have never heard of a lawyer with a rejection complex because of all the lawyer jokes. (Actually, you seminary guys have it pretty easy—lawyer jokes outnumber seminary jokes twenty to one.)

Christian Swartz did an extensive study of churches around the world—poor churches, rich churches, persecuted, nonpersecuted, large, small, and so forth. The results of this incredible study were published in his book *Natural Church Development.* Swartz was able to identify eight essential qualities that were present in healthy, growing churches. He discovered other things that I don't think he set out to find. One interesting one is that it is a negative factor for church growth to have a seminary-trained pastor. More than half the churches with professionally trained pastors were either declining in membership or not growing. Whereas with non-seminary-trained pastors, the church growth rate was higher.

CHAPTER 5

The Dumb Gringo: Funny Dumb, Little Dumb, Pretty Dumb, and Big Dumb

We all do dumb things. Some people do them more frequently than others. And of course there are different levels of dumb. For missions, I have divided dumbness into four basic categories: funny, little, pretty, and big. If we live in a foreign country or interact with a different culture, sooner or later (usually sooner) we'll mess up. We'll do something dumb. It is part of the learning process. Everyone who becomes a missionary will make cultural language mistakes.

Funny Dumb
When you commit funny dumb, it's OK. Of course, you need to have your pride on the cross when you are the object of the laughter. You'll have to learn to be humble and roll with the punches. Funny dumb is OK, but you don't want to dwell there. Your goal is to learn enough of the language and culture to keep the laughter of the nationals to a minimum. They expect you to be dumb for a while, but if your dumbness persists for years, the people won't respect you. The following are a few examples of funny dumb.

This is one that all missionaries in Latin America will commit sooner or later. In Spanish, the word for *sin* is *pecado*, and the word for *fish* is *pescado*. Yes, the day will come when you will boldly proclaim with great passion and conviction that Jesus died for your fish. In another instance, an American pastor was asked to help ordain twelve new ministers. The Spanish word *ordain* was slightly changed as it came out of his mouth, and he told each new minister, "I milk you in the name of Jesus."

A Mexican pastor, who has been a good friend of mine for twenty-four years, has shared some good ones. He told me about a young lady wanting to express her worship to God. She began to sing a song she had learned the night before. The song repeated the line "You have made me free," several times. In Spanish the word for *free* is *libre*. Unfortunately, she added a second *e* and was saying *liebre*, which means rabbit. For several minutes, she went on with great joy repeating, "Rabbit you have made me a rabbit." I often wonder if, after finishing the song, she had thanked God for making her a rabbit in Jesus.

A missionary I know took a visiting American with him to a village to conduct a church service. When they arrived, a family invited them to share a meal in their home. The visitor, wanting to be sociable, turned to the missionary and asked in a soft voice, "What is the word for *married*?" After the missionary told him, he then turned to ask the Mexican man next to him if he was married. In those few seconds, the word *casado* picked up a couple of extra letters, and he asked him if he was *castrado*, or castrated. Luckily, the missionary was there to bail him out.

Another person shared how a new missionary, as he was preaching, thought he was asking for all of the adults to raise their hands. No one raised their hands, and he declared, "I can't believe there are no adults here." He didn't figure out until later that he had mistakenly used *adulteros* (adulterers) in place of *adultos* (adults). If there were any adulterers present, I'll bet they were sweating bullets. It could have been worse. Some poor adulterer could have raised his hand. I can almost hear the new missionary saying, "God bless you, brother. I'm glad at least one person here is an adulterer."

One day, as I was traveling with Antonio Hernandez, an evangelist and friend from Saltillo, we began to exchange dumb gringo stories. He shared about an elderly missionary by the name of Gerry whom I have known for years. When she was still green, she was asked to conduct a church service in a village. They were showing a movie that night, so several unconverted men were attending the service. As is the custom, the men were standing along the back wall of the church. Sister Gerry, seeing several empty spaces on the benches, wanted to invite the men to come forward and be seated. In the old days before plastic chairs, most churches had wooden benches. I always thought they were designed for maximum discomfort. The backs were straight with no incline at all. As was the custom, all the women were seated on the benches. Sister Gerry, thinking that she was saying, "Everyone in the back," changed the word *todos* (everyone) to *toros* (bulls). That would have been bad enough, but it got worse. In Spanish the word for bench is *bancas*, but poor sister Gerry said *vacas*, which means cows. "Hey, you bulls back there, come on up—here's the cows!" Antonio and I laughed as he repeated it several times. I'll bet the women were terrified.

Larry, a friend of mine, was ministering to a Mexican man who wasn't a very good husband. Larry wanted to encourage him to be faithful to his wife, but instead of *fiel* he said *feo*, which means ugly. Larry told him, "God wants you to be ugly to your wife." On another occasion, someone asked Larry where he was from. He attempted to say, "I'm Larry. I live near Chicago." However, the word for *near*, *cerca*, was replaced by *circo*, which is *circus*. He also used the name Lorenzo for Larry, which can also mean *crazy* or *insane*. So what he said was, "I'm crazy from the Chicago circus." The good thing about Larry is he loves to tell this story on himself

One of my favorite funny dumb stories happened in Guatemala. Richard, a Mexican American pastor from southern California, was invited to preach at a conference held by a very strict Pentecostal group. Richard's message was "Don't Fear the Devil, Because You Have Power over Him." A good solid evangelical, charismatic, hermeneutically sound message. However, Richard made one fatal mistake that would catapult him to the top of my funny dumb list. For the word *Devil* he used the Mexican street slang word *chamuco*. "Brothers, don't fear the chamuco," he proclaimed. "You have power over the chamuco. The chamuco can't hurt you. You have to take authority over the chamuco." An older Guatemalan pastor worked his way up to the platform behind Richard and tugged on his shirt. "Brother," he whispered to Richard, "here in Guatemala *chamuco* is the private part of the woman."

What were the poor Guatemalans thinking for the first few minutes of his message? He had accomplished what few men ever achieve: Yes, he scored a perfect 10 in the funny dumb competition. To grasp the full impact of it, imagine you have a guest speaker in your nice little church and he uses street slang in English that is the equivalent of *chamuco* in Guatemala. I think you get my point. Second- and third-generation Mexican Americans can make some major mistakes because they assume they understand the culture and the language.

Little Dumb

Little dumb is the next level. In this category, there is usually no humor involved. You won't be the object of a good laugh. You will probably be the object of someone's anger or sorrow. Little dumb can cause some problems but is not fatal. It will not destroy someone's life, but it can cause relationship problems. It almost always is an innocent misunderstanding of the culture or expected behavior.

One example in Mexico is when you say to someone, "We're going out to eat. Would you like to come with us?" In Mexico that means, "I'm buying. Would you like to go eat?" We have had visiting church teams that invite nationals to eat out with them, resulting in nationals thinking the meal is paid for by those inviting. When no one picks up the tab, he or she is wondering why. If he or she is a working-class Mexican, the price of a meal in a nice restaurant can be beyond his or her budget. When they end up paying for their meal, it could be a day's wages. That is bad, but no permanent damage done.

Another problem came to my attention when a Mexican Christian asked me why brother Mark didn't like him. Mark had been making an annual trip to Mazatlán with another pastor from the Phoenix area for seven years. "I know Mark," I told Lorenzo. "I don't think he has anything against you." "He has something against me," Lorenzo insisted. I pressed on because I knew Mark, and I was sure he wasn't holding any grudges against the Mexican brother. "How do you know he doesn't like you?" I inquired. "Because he never shakes my hand," Lorenzo explained. The clash of two cultures once again. I explained to him that gringos don't always shake everyone's hand when they enter a room. Again, in Mexico, if you want to shun someone, you don't shake their hand when you enter a room or encounter them. Lorenzo, seeing things through his cultural lens, felt slighted. He was wondering what it was that Mark didn't like about him. And of course Mark didn't have a clue that trouble was brewing. I don't know what would have happened had I not been there as a bridge between two cultures.

My advice to gringos is, when in doubt, shake hands. You can't overshake, but you can undershake. When Mexicans show up at a meeting, they shake everyone's hand, and when they leave, they shake everyone's hand again. If you are talking to someone and he shakes your hand because he is leaving, but then you begin talking again, that requires a new shake.

There is often a lack of willingness as Americans to conform to the culture and standards of the country in which they are ministering. Simple observation will be our best teacher. I conform in a lot of ways that Americans don't notice. For example, I hardly ever wear shorts. Not because of some religious conviction; it is simply because most Mexicans don't wear shorts in Mazatlán even in the summer. Of course, that is changing constantly as they become more Westernized. I will change as they change.

One church that I know of would do an annual outreach to the poor in Mexico. They would go to a poor area and announce that at 11:00 a.m. they would be giving away bags of groceries. They had around a hundred bags to give away, but the two times I was with them, three hundred people showed up. Before giving away the food, the people had to wait in the hot sun to be evangelized. And of course, when asked to raise their hands if they wanted to receive Jesus, most did so thinking it might work to their advantage to get the free groceries. After the evangelism, they would try to line up the people to distribute the food, but it was total chaos. People were pushing and shoving and fighting for position. Then the food would run out. Two hundred people gave an hour or two of their time waiting in the hot sun being evangelized, expecting a bag of groceries that never materialized. The result was a mixed effect. One hundred happy people and two hundred disappointed ones.

This church did other foolish things as well. They tried to line the children up to give them candy. They quickly lost control and were surrounded by kids trying to grab the candy, but instead of putting the candy away, they began to throw it. Of course the children charged after the candy, some getting knocked to the ground as they did so. They were lucky that no children were injured. I mentioned to those that were throwing the candy that they shouldn't be doing so, but the damage was done. These churches had been doing outreaches for several years, and I didn't feel the liberty after one visit to tell them they were dumb gringos.

In Mazatlán, we receive a lot of church groups, and we take them out to the poor areas to give away free bags of groceries. However, there are two things that we do to help us avoid the problems that I have already mentioned: (1) We always separate evangelism from the giving, and (2) we maintain order and a sense of fairness when we hand out whatever it is that we are giving to people.

Whenever you have too much evangelism connected with giving something away, you are sending the wrong message to the people. It looks like you are using a gift to the poor to entice them to convert. Those who are antievangelical will use it against the church. I have heard people comment about Christians trying to buy converts. Of course, the anti-Christian crowd will criticize anything they can, but let's not give them any ammunition to use against us. When we do an outreach in Mazatlán, we'll give away food in the morning, usually without doing overt evangelism. Typically, as people gather to receive their gift, we have teams ready to offer to pray for those who have a need and desire for prayer. The response is usually very positive, with many folks asking to be ministered to. As the prayer teams are ministering, evangelism often occurs, but without the appearance of enticing people.

The other thing we do to ensure order and a sense of fairness is hand out numbered tickets that are exchanged for the bag of groceries or whatever it is that we are giving away. By handing out tickets, we can target the poorest people in the area. By using tickets, and numbered ones at that, the crowd problem is controlled. When the people see that everyone is being called by number, they don't need to mob you out of fear that the food will run out before you get to them. Of course, we assure them that everyone with a ticket will receive the handout, but they won't receive anything until we get to their number. We have no control problems. Do more people show up than we have food for? Yes, they do, but since they weren't promised anything, their expectations are low. Sometimes people with tickets don't show up to claim their gift. In that case, we distribute what is left to those without tickets. Another advantage of using the tickets is that people are not able to sneak back in line again, which happens when tickets are not used.

We had a church group visit from Brownsville, Texas. I didn't know it at the time, but the people in charge of doing outreaches for their church across the border in Mexico were on the team. They had become discouraged because whenever they went to Mexico to give things away, they would lose control and get mobbed by the people. Ministry to the poor had become something they dreaded. After working with us in Mazatlán, they adopted our methods and had the same results as we did. Other groups that work with the poor in the United States have also borrowed our methods and have reported positive results as well.

What gringos don't understand is that the Mexicans are not always going to correct them. They show up with their program and money, and the nationals go along with them. Unlike American culture, Mexican culture is nonconfrontational. They will allow you to do things your way instead of confronting you and telling you're a dumb gringo. It took me a while to learn this cultural lesson. I have had Mexican pastors share with me concerns and dislikes for what some American pastors were doing, but later, when meeting with these same American pastors about whom they had expressed concern in private, the Mexican pastors kept silent. I waited for them to bring up the issues they had expressed to me, but it never happened. When I mentioned a couple of the points, they sat there motionless as though they had never heard those things before.

If you observe, you can see nonconfrontationalism all through the culture, sometimes in subtle ways. Here is an example: There is a restaurant in Mazatlán that is popular to both locals and tourists. They are known for their good desserts, and before you finish your meal, the dessert cart will have made it twice to your table with the question, "Would you like some dessert?" At times I have dined there with a mixed group of both Americans and Mexicans. Whenever the girl with the dessert cart would ask if we would like something, the Americans who didn't want any dessert would say, "No, thank you. I don't want any." But the Mexicans who don't want any dessert never say, "No, thank you." They always reply, "Not right now, thank you." They don't want to tell you no so they tell you, "Not right now."

When I was still a rookie missionary, I went to a town in the mountains to show a Christian movie. The town had a population of around thirty thousand but had no evangelical churches. Mario and I were going around and inviting people to the movie. We entered a small store and invited the girl behind the counter to the movie. "I'll be there," she replied. However, I had not told her the time or location of the event. I asked, "Are you sure you are going?" "Oh, yes, I'll be there," she answered. I asked her again, subtly setting my trap. "What time and where are you going?" I asked. "What time did you say?" she nervously asked me. "I didn't say what time," I replied. I did not understand the culture yet. Mexicans never say a definitive no. It is always, "Sure, I'll come by later." After we left the store, Mario told me, "If I had done that, she would have been angry, but an American can get away with it." I still hadn't figured out the nonconfrontational way that Mexican nationals operate. I had graduated from funny dumb to little dumb. Now my goal was to avoid the big dumb category

Another experience I had a couple years later would move me closer to cultural enlightenment. I had planted a church in the town of Calera and left a Mexican national in charge. One day five men from the church showed up at my house in Fresnillo, telling me about several problems that they thought were serious. They were very upset with the pastor, the direction that the church was going, and recent affairs. The pastor had a sister who had just moved to town. Her daughter ran away from home, and he took her in. The police showed up at the church with a paddy wagon and threatened to arrest the pastor. They were upset about the bad publicity the church was getting and wanted me to intervene immediately. The family whose daughter had run away also sought me out. As I investigated, it was obvious that there was no sexual abuse or anything else that would warrant taking in an underaged girl. I would later learn that the pastor's clan had a history of conflict. I called a meeting, and we met with the pastor. However, when I asked the five men from the church what they had to say, no one wanted to say anything in front of the pastor. *El gato* (the cat) had got their tongues. They wanted me to bring up all of the complaints. They wanted the pastor confronted, but they didn't want to do it.

Over the years, you would be surprised by all the things I have heard from the Mexican nationals in private conversations when they express their true feelings about some of the Americans. I can't tell an American pastor or missions leader that "So-and-So feels this way about you or about the way you do things." If he were to go to the Mexican national and ask him, the national would probably claim to not remember saying that, or he would say, "I feel" and then reword his private criticism to be less confrontational. It would look like I was making up stuff.

Please don't get the impression that the Mexican nationals sit around talking about the American pastors all of the time. That is not the case. However, over the years, on occasions, I've heard them express their true feelings, both negative and positive. My point is, because of the nonconfrontational nature of their culture, unless you speak their language and have lived with them for several years, they probably won't express their true feelings to you.

Pretty Dumb

When I was still a green missionary living in central Mexico, we put together a basketball team and joined the newly formed league. At that time, basketball was still fairly new in central Mexico and was just beginning to gain a little popularity. No good local basketball players had been developed yet. Jack, a friend of mine, had moved to Mexico to help us in our missions work. I am about 5'9", and back in those days (early 1980s), I was taller than the average Mexican. Jack was 6'3" or 6'4", so he was considered to be a pretty big guy. We showed up for the first game ready to run and gun. Everyone on the opposing team was shorter than me. That meant that Jack was really big. He dominated the boards. Our shorter opponents couldn't seem to get a rebound or a lay-up with Jack in the post. It was a massacre. The final score was something like 64 to 20. Somewhere along the way we had forgotten that our goal was to use the basketball league as a means to reach the community and share the love of Christ. We were young and obviously not too bright at that time. We got caught up with the emotion of the game, and our competitive spirit got the best of us.

At that point, we should have gone home and let the dust settle. But it seems we were not content with having achieved the highest rating of little dumb—no, not us. We had to push the envelope a little more. Someone came up with the brilliant idea that we should go tell the team that we just slaughtered how much God loves them. Have you ever tried to tell someone that you and God love them after you just stomped them into the ground, and in public at that? Needless to say, no converts were made that night. We had graduated from little dumb and catapulted ourselves into the pretty dumb category. When it finally dawned on us what we had accomplished, we were repentant. We decided not to continue in the basketball league. What we didn't find out until later is that when we didn't show up for the next game, some of the locals claimed to represent our church and continued in the league with our church name.

The big dumb category is so rich, so significant, it deserves several of its own sections.

"I Will Not Blend In"

For many years, we held our annual pastors' retreat near the city of Durango in a small Methodist retreat center. The conference has always been a special time because of the close fellowship. We always did our own cooking and left time for games and fun. Some of the best times would happen after the official meeting or class when someone would pick up a guitar and spontaneous worship would break out. Our teaching was done in the dining room. Only a counter top separated the dining room and the kitchen so those who had kitchen duty never missed the classes.

With so much close fellowship, games, and sporting activities, we all learned a lot about each other. Our little quirks would show. Sometimes we would learn more than we wanted to know, and other times we would reveal more about ourselves than we desired. During our break time, we would play a game that we call volley pong. To play volley pong, you lower the net to waist height and use a ball lighter than a volleyball. Most people think I invented the game because I made up the rules. We never picked teams; we would simply announce, "We need eight on each side" and in a minute or two the teams would be formed. Near the end of one retreat, one of the leaders told me, "Last year I lost every game I played. It dawned on me that I was never on your team. This year, whenever the teams were forming, I would run over to the side where you were." He then explained, "You don't like to lose, and whenever you are losing, you start motivating everyone on your team to play harder and not give up." He went on to add, "Besides that, you're the only one who knows all the rules and I figure that works to your advantage as well." My competitive spirit and my dislike of losing were revealed.

I have met some missionaries who might as well have worn a six-foot high red hat saying, "I will not blend in." Back in the early 1990s, a couple from the United States joined us in central Mexico. The nationals never seemed to warm up to them. The problem became more evident when they attended our pastor's retreat near Durango. During breakfast, they had their own food. Their kids didn't like the breakfast so they gave them cereal and juice. Then came the pills—vitamins, supplements, and so forth. It looked like they were going to open a pharmacy. It was like they had a flashing light on their head stating, "I won't blend in." Many of the pastors were poor working-class, so the contrast was obvious. They could have used some wisdom and taken their vitamins and supplements back in their room.

They never did understand the principle of becoming like the people whom you are called to minister to. At least, you do not want to stand out. I am not advocating a strict policy of imitation. I am saying blend in a natural way without overdoing it. If nobody wears shorts in the region you are in, then do not be the first one to do so. This couple would do other things that would draw attention to how different they were. For example, they had two preteen boys, and when they were going to make a decision, the boys would have to agree with them, or they would not do it. For some reason, they would make those things known to the nationals who in turn would think they were weird. The Mexicans never did connect with them. After a while, they moved on. I don't think they had a clue they were the ones to blame for the lack of acceptance by the Mexicans.

The MacMahon Factor,
or Allow Me to Contradict Myself

Even though it is important to blend into the culture in which you are called to work and to treat the nationals as equals, if this is done in an unnatural and mechanical way, the end result may not be the fruit you want. These things must flow out of the love and humility that are part of our soul and character.

Years ago I met Dennis MacMahon. In our lifetimes we meet countless people, most of whom we forget ever having met. Not so with Dennis. If you met Dennis MacMahon, you would never forget him. He was one of the most unique characters I have ever met. I first met Dennis at the Berean Christian bookstore in Peoria, Illinois, where he worked. Dennis had thick glasses, which I never remember having seen clean. His clothes always seemed to be wrinkled, as though he had slept in them. The person accompanying me was talking to Dennis, and during the course of the conversation, he mentioned a prayer request, asking Dennis to remember it in prayer. I expected Dennis to conduct himself as a normal Christian and say, "Of course I'll pray for you," and then ten minutes later forget about it.

That wasn't how Dennis operated, as I immediately found out. He grabbed my friend's hand and said, "Let's pray." Right there on the spot in front of the other customers, he prayed for the need. I found out that you should never ask Dennis to pray for you unless you meant that you wanted to be prayed for right there on the spot. It didn't matter where you were—on a street corner, in a restaurant, or even in the lobby at church. I later found out that some of the customers at the bookstore didn't like Dennis praying. What a crime, praying in a Christian bookstore.

Dennis had a Bible study once a week in his apartment. Even the Bible study was unique. It was attended by a broad social range of people: professionals, intellectuals, middle class, ex-hippies, college students, and others. No one taught the study. They would listen to a tape, and if at any time anyone wanted to make a comment, they would stop the tape, and a time of discussion would follow.

Well, you guessed it. After a while, Dennis felt called to Mexico. After what I have written about becoming a part of the culture and blending in, you are probably thinking, "Here is the most unpromising candidate possible. This guy can't keep from standing out in his own culture. What is he going to look like in another culture? He will especially stand out." One thing about which I always counsel North Americans is that you don't want to go to a foreign country and stand out any more than is necessary. This is good advice, and I stand by it. How would the Mexicans respond to this walking attraction?

Dennis rolled into Fresnillo with his old van packed full of his philosophy books and began his missionary adventure. In a short time, the Mexicans took to him. All the Mexican pastors I knew loved having Dennis around. His passionate spirituality and sincere love and respect for the Mexican people overruled any potential negative effect of his appearance. He didn't treat the nationals as equals simply because he had read a book on the failures of the colonial missionaries. He didn't have a list of rules saying, "Now treat the nationals as equals and don't rule over them." He didn't need the list because he never contracted CMC.

The fact that Dennis was always broke actually helped him with the poor working-class Mexicans. They had never seen a gringo who was possibly poorer than they were. Sometimes they would ask Dennis to take them somewhere in his van for a church service. Almost always, the Mexican pastor would have to contribute for the gas. They loved it. They had no trouble seeing Dennis as an equal. After all, he actually needed them. He wasn't a highly educated seminarian with a good salary, backed by a mission agency. He was like them. He was one of them even though he stood out like a

Christmas tree and was an intellectual.

Unfortunately, Dennis's missionary career was short-lived. He was engaged to a girl who would never consent to a missions career. We all saw that, but Dennis was hoping she would eventually be convinced. But she wasn't.

I do stand by my policy to blend in to the culture where you serve, but there are always exceptions to the rule. The MacMahon factor is an exception. After all, it's truly an issue of your own heart. You can blend in 'til the cows come home, but if the heart's not right, it will all be in vain.

Allow Me To Contradict Myself Again

I firmly stand by my policy to try to blend in and become a part of the culture. That should be our starting point and assumption. However, the world has not only changed radically since the time of Hudson Taylor and Roland Allen but also since the 1980s when Dennis MacMahon was in Mexico. Because of worldwide communications, American movies that are seen around the world, satellite television, e-mail, Web sites, and many other things, people around the globe have been exposed to many different cultures (mostly American). It is no longer a shock to see someone dressed differently. It is no longer a factor of the magnitude that it was in the 1800s in China when Western dress could be a major obstacle.

Each country will have to be examined individually. You will need to take into consideration the social or cultural group to which you will be ministering within each country. There will be instances in which it will be advantageous to look like an American and other times when it will not. If you are young man, in certain places it might be best to keep your earrings, while in other places, it would be a negative factor. For example, if you are called to work on a college campus, that would require a dress code totally different than if you were sent to minister among poor farmers (*campesinos*) in Mexico. These are the questions you'll have to ask yourself. But before asking these questions, you need to put everything on the altar—all of your dress standards, ideas, hair styles, earrings, Nike tennis shoes, and all the rest. Then, allow the Holy Spirit to tell you what you can take back. True passion will cause you to do this!

Don't be a dumb gringo and stand out more than you have to.

An example of the danger of eliminating the cultural bridge as a missionary happened in Latin America. An American pastor who was the overseer for missions in Latin American for his denomination was invited to speak at a gathering in which several pastors were present. He showed up in his old faded blue jeans. He stood out like a Ku Klux Klansman at a Nation of Islam meeting. Most of the Latino pastors wore neckties.

It is not necessary for people to make mistakes so they can personally learn a lesson. If this pastor's church had a missionary on the field, he would have been informed beforehand that his dress was inappropriate. Why would you want to make a mistake that could easily have been avoided? Avoid as many mistakes as possible. There will be enough mistakes to deal with without any unnecessary ones. If you are not smart enough to figure out beforehand that dress standards are different in Latin America than they are in the United States, then how do you expect to pick up other cultural differences that are not as obvious?

"Oops! I Changed Your Message!"

In the 1980s, we began to minister to the poor. I had been working with a group of pilots who would fly in doctors and dentists, and we would set up field clinics. Their ministry was very fruitful, we enjoyed working with them, and we looked forward to their visits. However, one ministry trip didn't turn out as we expected. The two small planes arrived on schedule, but on this trip, they had brought a few extra people. The girlfriend of one of the pilots had gone to the airport to see her boyfriend off and on the spur of the moment decided to join them. She was a very good-looking girl and arrived wearing a very revealing dress—completely out of place for central Mexico in the 1980s. Back then, just seeing a gringo was a major event and would turn heads. Imagine the effect of a hot-looking gringa with a short, short dress. Since she came at the spur of the moment, she didn't pack a suitcase.

That was bad enough, but it got worse. One of the dentists was a big ol' guy who reminded me of the old cartoon character Baby Huey. He was wearing shorts. Up to that time I had never seen anyone with shorts on in central Mexico. Unfortunately, he wasn't finished with making himself stand out from the local population. He also had on a floral Hawaiian shirt and yes, to my amazement a big camera hanging around his neck. You could literally see him coming a mile away.

But the biggest blow was yet to come and would catch me off-guard. Two other men had accompanied the pilots and dentists on the mission trip. The team leader explained that they were members of a church in Houston that supported their ministry. The next morning we headed out to a village a couple of hours away from Fresnillo. We planned on holding the dental clinic until 4 or 5 in the afternoon and afterward having an evangelistic service. There were no evangelical churches in the village. The pilot in charge of the ministry asked me if the guys from Houston could preach the evening services and if I would interpret for them. "Sure," I told him, "I'd be glad to do it."

What I didn't yet know is that the two men were into what was known back then as the "Prosperity Doctrine." The prosperity preachers would put an unhealthy emphasis on the Scriptures that mentioned anything about God wanting to bless us materially or financially. They taught that every Christian could prosper financially and that poverty was a curse and not the will of God. Some of them taught what was labeled the "Name It and Claim It" doctrine. You could claim by faith a new car or house or whatever it was that you desired. Of course, there were different levels of the prosperity teaching; some went to the extremes, while others were more balanced.

Unfortunately the gentlemen from Houston were extremely poor in the wisdom department. They didn't seem to understand that non-Christians needed to hear the Gospel, not the prosperity doctrine. Anyway, I was interpreting for one of them and expecting a good "Jesus died for you" message, when out of his mouth flowed the Name It and Claim It doctrine. What was I to do? Here was a group of people that had no understanding that salvation is a gift of God that is obtained by grace when we believe the Gospel, and they were being told how to prosper financially.

In extraordinary circumstances, one must rise to the occasion and do extraordinary things. Yes, I rose to the occasion. I didn't hold back. I had never attempted before to do what I was about to do. But it had to be done and I was available. I opened my mouth and I changed his message. As he was preaching about the curse of poverty, I was preaching Christ crucified. I never did tell him. I didn't consider him to be in a need-to-know situation. My mission was accomplished. I saved him from being a dumb gringo. Well, that is not completely true. He *was* a dumb gringo. However, I saved him from being exposed as a dumb gringo to all the Mexican Christians helping us on the outreach. I was the only one who knew how dumb he was. He earned the highest rating of big dumb.

CHAPTER 6

Money and Missions

Can money hinder missions? Can money hurt missions? Can money seriously damage missions? Can money rob initiative from nationals? Can money cause division in missions churches? Can money bless mission work? Can money help expand the work? Can money accelerate growth? Can money be given without the nationals losing ownership or initiative?

The answer to all of these questions is yes! Money can both help and hinder, bless and curse, accelerate and slow down the work. I heard of one missions group who did a study and found out that the more money they invested in a work, the less effective it was. I have no doubt that their analysis was correct. Evangelical Colonial and Reformed Evangelical Colonial missionaries, I believe, will have the most difficulty being effective with money. I also think that those who suffer from colonial missionary complex will have some difficulties being effective—especially those with severe CMC.

At this point it might be good to state what we *don't* want to do with money:

1. We don't want to create dependence. We don't want churches or national pastors or workers who develop a dependence on us in order for the work to continue.
2. We don't want national churches always looking to us to meet their financial needs.

We want our financial assistance to somehow translate into establishing missions work, church planting, advancing the kingdom of God, or accelerating church growth. Of course, we should look at our overall giving and discern if it is truly making a difference.

Let's focus on something more tangible: buildings. To build or not to build—that is the question. Should we build church buildings, help the nationals build churches, or offer no financial assistance at all? That's a good question, and there's no easy universal answer. The answer can be yes or no to each question, depending on the situation and the compelling factors.

Roland Allen and other writers have given a blanket answer saying we should not build churches. Allen said something to the effect that if Muslims can build their mosques without outside help, why should we do it for Christians? And of course, he based everything on the Book of Acts. I believe that because Allen was part of a colonial-type missions group that was ineffective in using money to advance the kingdom of God, he was prone to be reactionary when presenting his views. After all, he never saw a successful model.

Allen also incorrectly analyzed the money issue in his observation that Muslims don't need outside help. For example, a Muslim country is usually just that—all Muslim. Therefore, the pool for raising funds is large. The area in which I work in is over 95 percent Catholic, and some of the poorest areas of town (colonias) have no Catholic churches. Why do you think that is? Because of the extreme poverty, the money pool is too low to raise the necessary money to build a church. Some of the people who are most receptive to the Gospel live in these poor colonias. If the Catholics, who are a 95 percent majority, can't build a church in these areas, why would you expect a 5 percent minority to do it?

What are the options then? Not to establish a work in the extremely poor colonias? Or perhaps you are saying, "Why do you need a building? In the Book of Acts, they didn't build any churches." A building is important for several reasons. Like it or not, a building is an important part of modern Christianity in most countries. A building says that you are there to stay. It communicates permanence.

Years ago, when I lived in central Mexico, I would make a two-hour trip over rough terrain to a village without running water or electricity. The reason for the trip was to visit a young school-teacher named Mario who had been converted in one of my city crusades. I would spend two or three hours, one day a week, teaching him the Bible. I saw a lot of potential in him and felt it was important to invest time teaching him (later he would run a Bible school and develop teaching materials for others).

On these trips, I would sometimes take a generator and show Christian movies to the people who lived in the village. Mario and I would take turns preaching the Gospel. One day, a young lady approached Mario and said she wanted to become a Christian, but she would not do so unless we were committed enough to the village to eventually build a church. Of course, Mario explained that a building wasn't necessary to be a Christian. He told her we had no such plans. She knew that his tenure would be up in a few months and he would be transferred to a better school. To our knowledge, she never made a commitment to Christ. This experience remains vivid in my memory. This young lady didn't care about a fancy church building. She knew she would have to suffer for the Gospel and didn't want to be abandoned. She knew a building would communicate commitment.

Another reason a building may be necessary is for the purpose of reaching children. We like to go into extremely poor areas and build a children's feeding center. According to official studies, 48 percent of Mexican children are undernourished. This presents us with an open door to minister. Not only do we feed the kids; we give them a Bible class as well. Anywhere from eighty to three hundred kids will show up. "Why not hold the class and feeding in the street?" you ask. We usually start in the street. However, for six to seven months of the year it's so hot that we can't do much outside. To effectively minister year-round, we need a roof. I'll explain our strategies in more detail later.

It sounds good on paper: Let the nationals build their own buildings. If your mission can plant churches without helping to build buildings, then go for it. I am for following either approach as long as it is effective. I have personally seen both sides. I have seen empty church buildings because a missionary, who had money and only a few converts, hurried in and built a church, which never grew afterward. Some missionaries were supported by groups or churches that measured success by the building of churches. These supporters were too building focused and had trouble accepting that a work had been successful unless a church building had been built. This put unhealthy pressure on the missionary to build buildings so that he would be considered effective and not lose his financial support. Some missionaries would yield to the pressure and build churches that should never have been built. Some of these churches would shut down and discontinue holding services.

When I lived in central Mexico, I was asked by a national pastor if I would take over a church building that had been closed for years. He explained the situation and told me he had no one in his organization to start the church there. I accepted and took over the property. This town of forty thousand people where the church property was located was very hostile to the bearers of the Gospel. No evangelical church plant had ever survived. The church building that we inherited wasn't much. It only held about twenty people, but it was on a great piece of land. In about a year, we grew out of the small facility and built a larger sanctuary. The poor brethren, with much sacrifice, paid for most of the construction cost. A few years later, we broke off a group and planted a church in the neighboring town. Actually, the two towns had grown together and were separated by the highway. Even though the original building had looked like a wasted investment in an abandoned church, it would have been much more difficult for us to have started without the advantage of the property. The second church plant might never have happened. Starting out with land and a small building accelerated our church-planting efforts.

Another factor made it important to have a building even before the church started. That was the persecution factor. In those days, persecution could be very severe. Once, while doing a follow-up after one of our tent meetings, we were surprised that nearly all of the addresses of those who came forward were incorrect. If it had been just a few, we would have assumed that they made a mistake when giving us their addresses. But our great powers of deduction told us that something was up! They didn't want us to go to their houses. If their neighbors found out that they had attended an evangelical event, it would have meant persecution. That's why, under certain conditions, a church can't be started by first having home groups. The persecution can be too intimidating. In this case it was safer to go to the building and hope that your neighbor didn't find out. Later, when converts were stronger, we started home groups.

I have also seen the opposite, where church growth accelerates after having a church building donated. Before I arrived in Mazatlán, teams of Americans came and built twelve churches for the Assembly of God denomination. Instead of creating a Christian welfare system, it thrust the Assemblies of God ahead. They are now the dominant church group here. One of the churches they built has now grown to be the largest in this city. So the question is no longer "Should we build it?" but "Will it accelerate and advance the kingdom of God?" Four years after having eight churches built for them, the Assemblies of God grew to sixteen churches.

Money and missions will also be a danger area for modern missions, especially for the "do missions differently" group. Even with my limited exposure to the world of missions, I've seen far too many bad and harmful things done with money. Even as I write, in this area where I work, a group of American Christians are building an orphanage. Two weeks before I found out about this new project, I met a couple who have a foundation in the United States whose sole purpose is to support orphans. They told me if I decide to start an orphanage some day, they would like to help fund it. I told them the truth: that where I work there are already too many orphanages. And, besides that, most of them aren't really orphanages. Some of them have no orphans at all. Since orphans aren't readily available, these groups look for poor families whom they feel are not able to properly care for their children. They then offer to place the children in their orphanage and educate them. During the school break, the children go home for the summer. Recently, a visiting American lady went to visit the orphanage she was supporting and found no children present. She asked me what was up, and I had to explain that the children are not really orphans and that they go home during the summer. Americans with noble intensions have no clue about the true need. If they had a new breed missionary in the field, they could avoid wasting God's money.

Never forget that money can be the biggest obstacle to missions. You may be handling money in a very foolish way without being aware of it. You who are missions directors and coordinators residing in the United States need to accept that you are not the most qualified person to be investing God's money in the mission field. One of the biggest challenges for twenty-first-century missions will be how to handle money. Being effective with money on the mission field will require more than reading the latest books on missions or even the reading the classics on missions. We will all make mistakes with money, but we want to keep the mistakes to a minimum and learn from them quickly. Just because we have money doesn't ensure success in our missions endeavors. Money alone will accomplish very little, and it can even do great harm.

"Oops! I Planted an English Church in Mexico!"

In 1996, we moved to Mazatlán to plant a church. Mazatlán is a resort city on the west coast of Mexico. One of our strategies is to first plant a church that reaches middle-class and professional-class people. By doing so, it is easier to raise up a self-supporting church. It is important to reach this class of people when starting out. I decided to ask one of the five-star hotels if they would let me use their conference center for Sunday services at no charge. However, I knew that if I told them that I was planting a church to reach locals, the response would be negative. Mazatlán depends on American and Canadian tourists, so I told them I needed the conference center for church services that would be open to tourists. The hotel manager liked the idea of tourists coming to his hotel and gave me the conference center for free. The truth of the matter is that I had no plans or desire to minister to Canadians and Americans. I was using them as an excuse to get the facility for free to plant the Spanish church. I didn't realize that I had set something in motion that would alter the way we would operate in Mazatlán.

Soon a respectable number of gringos were attending the Sunday morning service at Los Sabalos beach resort. We would sing just enough songs in English to keep their attention. I preached in Spanish, and my wife interpreted the message into English for the tourists. For two years we met at the resort hotel, during which time the English service continued to grow. During what they call the high season (December through March), the number of tourists attending the service would go up. Then, we would start into the low season and numbers would decline. All that time, I gave virtually no attention to the gringo church.

After two years, we grew weary of carrying equipment to the second floor of the conference center. It was especially difficult during the hot months. By the time we got everything carried up, we would be soaking wet. Also, in the low season when there weren't many tourists attending the service, the hotel wouldn't turn on the air conditioning until service time. By then, we were all sweating like pigs. We decided that it was time to rent a place for our church. We found a place in the Golden Zone (the main tourist area) and negotiated an incredible price. Since both the Spanish and English groups were growing and because our new facility was smaller, we separated the English and Spanish services.

Suddenly, the English service began to grow more. I don't remember when it finally hit me that, "Oops, I have an English church. I am the pastor of an English church. How could this happen? I didn't plan this. I never visit any of them." In the beginning, I didn't even socialize with the attendees. Many of the members would be in Mazatlán from November through April. I found myself getting attached to them. I couldn't believe it. Then I discovered that they were interested in helping with our ministry to the poor. Suddenly, generous donors were helping us build feeding centers. I was thrust into the most challenging stage in my mission career: how to handle the finances that were coming in without hindering the work or diminishing the initiative of the nationals. I would draw on every ounce of my twenty years of experience to steer this course and avoid major disaster. Books alone never could have prepared me for this challenge. I was to be taxed to the maximum.

One of the things that I learned years before would be my guiding principle. That is, never support national workers or pastors personally with outside money. In other words, do not give regular financial support (salaries) to nationals. That's probably the one thing that has hindered the development of the national churches more than anything else. Once a Mexican church finds out that gringos are supporting the pastor, it kills their initiative for giving. "Why should I sacrifice?" they reason. "The gringos are rich anyway." When people don't support their own pastor and church, they never feel ownership. I am also convinced that giving is one of the things that releases the power of God. By taking that act away from church members, we are robbing them of blessings. My policy for years has been to never start nationals with a salary from outside money. (I know some ministries in India promote paying nationals with outside money. I have never been to India, so I don't know how effective they really are.)

In ministering in Mexico, I began to explain my philosophy to the English church. They understood and accepted it. Then, every opportunity that presented itself, I would communicate it to the nationals. In meetings with church staff or national workers, I would explain that the Gringos were willing to build the children's feeding centers, but we had to maintain them. We needed to take advantage of the buildings and start churches. I explained that the gringos were willing to build the buildings, but we had to support our own pastors. I would state it in different ways as often as I could: "If the gringos see that we're maintaining the buildings, they will build more for us." I have probably repeated this message hundreds if not thousands of times. Just a couple of times won't do. You need to state it and restate it.

The stakes are high. Money alone can't make things happen, but it sure can mess things up. A work can't be built on money because if the money dries up, the work will soon collapse. Depending on the circumstances and the compelling factors, a building (money) can either hinder or advance the work. There will be times when not helping will hinder a more rapid expansion of the work. Knowing when, where, and how to use money will be one of the key issues if modern missions are to be successful.

As I already mentioned, financially supporting national pastors can be a major hindrance to the development of national churches. Even if you tell the national pastor not to tell anyone that you are supporting him, eventually word will get out. Other struggling pastors or those wanting to be pastors will be inclined to expect help from the gringos as well. When placed in this position, some- times the nationals will try too hard to become friends with one of the gringos, hoping that it will result in financial assistance. If you insist on supporting national pastors, please do so with an exit plan. Give the pastor full support the first year. The second year begin to reduce the amount of support each month. The third year he should be on his own. I don't recommend this course of action, but if you choose it, you should put everything in writing to avoid problems. Later I will explain how to help a national pastor without handing out money.

Let me share a practical example of how financial assistance can be effective in accelerating the work. One of the pressing needs in many of our churches is in the area of worship and music. Since we are continually planting new churches, we not only need more pastors, but more and better worship leaders and musicians. We had some worship leaders who could play the guitar very well, but with some songs they would have trouble starting the song with their voice in the same key as the song. Others needed to improve their playing ability. The needs were many and varied. We planned an eleven-day intensive worship school. All of those that wanted to attend the school were from the poor working class. Some were pastors of small poor churches; others were volunteer worship leaders and musicians just barely making a living.

One man, named Jorge, was a self-employed, working-class poor man with a wife and four kids. Several nights a week, he sets up a table in the tourist zone and paints ocean scenes on tiles to sell. He makes just enough money to get by. One day, I was informed that he had run out of propane gas at his house and his wife was unable to cook. Tourism was down, and he hadn't sold many tiles. Jorge is one of the worship leaders in the main church as well as in a branch church. He gives a lot of his time to the worship ministry. There was no way he could stop working for two weeks and pay to go to our worship school. We gave him a scholarship to cover the tuition and transportation to our school. Even with that, it was a great sacrifice giving up two weeks of income.

Several of the nationals were in the same predicament. One of our men that needed the training and wanted to attend couldn't give up two weeks of work because of some bills that he had. The majority of those who needed the training would not have been able to attend without our assistance. That would have slowed down progress and hindered our development. This is a perfect example of how to help. We didn't hand them money; we supplied what they needed. No one got the impression that the Americans were giving them money.

After we got to the location of the school, I told the two pastors in charge of the school about the limited finances available for meals. They figured out how to do some budget meals for eleven days. They found all kinds of ways to cut costs. We didn't have enough spoons and forks for the students, so they reused plastic throw-away spoons. Some of the meals weren't that great, but I ate the same meals as they did. That's part of being a missionary. We did the training at a cost of twenty-five dollars per student. That included thirty-five meals provided for each one. By doing it at such a low cost, it will be something that they can do on their own when we are no longer with them.

It's Good to Be Broke

Sometimes it is good to be broke, and it is good for the nationals to see you broke. A local Mazatlán building contractor and developer was impressed with our feeding centers and our ministry to the poor. He offered to build us a fifty by seventy foot community center in a poor colonia. He would do everything but the metal roof. The roof would be our responsibility. Since he had his own construction company, he finished his part rather quickly. Our man in charge of overseeing all of our projects contacted me. "The contractor wants you to get the roof on so we can hold a dinner for the colonia," he informed me. "I'm broke," I replied, "we can't do anything right now." Wes, a member of our English church congregation, is always concerned about the colonia works and is always ready to help in any way that he can. "It's important that we get the roof on," he told me. "I can loan you the money." I said, "Thanks, Wes, for your offer, but it's sometimes good to be broke." I met with our construction overseer, and we arranged credit with the roofing company. Soon word got around that we were broke and operating on credit. You need to understand that people in third world countries see us as wealthy. At times they get the idea that Americans have a lot of money to throw around. If you are not wise and careful with the way you handle and spend money, you can create and reinforce this perception.

Don't Show the Money

One of our Mazatlán wintertime church members is a man from Alaska named Stewart. "Stew," as I call him, is a commercial real estate agent. He is a mover and a shaker and very committed to the Lord and missions. Even though he's not retired, he takes two to three months off during the winter to help us in Mazatlán. He and his wife have a lot of faith and trust in the Lord.

One example that showed me his incredible commitment happened as we were driving along the street that follows the beach. Earlier that day, Stew had found out that his secretary decided to quit without telling him. She just locked up his office and didn't return. Stew was contacting some of his regular clients when he discovered it. One of his clients had gone by the office twice and found it closed. He wanted to list a hospital, and since Stewart's office was closed, he went to another agent. The hospital sold in a couple of days. The realtor's commission, if I remember correctly, was thirty-five thousand dollars. As we were driving along, Stew explained what had happened and the money that he had lost on the deal. "I'm down here serving the Lord, and it cost me a thirty-five thousand dollars commission," he sighed. I'm thinking, "Boy, he's going to be depressed for a while." Then it was like he flipped a switch. "It doesn't matter," he said. "God will bless me in some other way." That was it. It was over. I never heard him talk about it again. I was amazed. "Boy, do I have a good sermon illustration," I thought.

The following year Stew and his family returned to Mazatlán. He had raised some money and was anxious to get some things done. He wanted to get all of our church vehicles painted the same color with signs on them. Jorge, one of our faithful volunteers, has a van that he uses a lot for church work. Stewart pulled out a huge wad of money and asked Jorge what it would cost to get it painted. "Get that window fixed as well," Stewart said as he peeled off money. Later I explained to Stewart the perception he had created in Jorge: "I've got a lot of money, and I'm looking for places to spend it." "The money that you pulled out represented six months' to a year's salary to him," I said. To a poor Mexican, that was a huge sum of money. Putting it into context, let's say that you make sixty thousand a year. Some guy pulls out thirty thousand dollars in cash and asks, "What will it cost to have you do something for me?" What would your perception be? A lot of Mexicans only make one thousand a year. When they see you pull out a year's wages, what do you expect them to think? To his credit, Stewart learned the lesson and never did it again.

However, the genie was out of the bottle, and it would take a little while to get it back in. Word got around, and a couple days later, one of our pastors told Stewart that he needed a PA system. With the language barrier, Stewart thought that he needed a couple hundred bucks. He told the pastor to go downtown, get some prices, and get back to him. What Stewart was trying to tell him was to get the prices but that Stewart himself would not make the decision. However, his Spanish wasn't all that good yet, and the pastor thought he was supposed to bring me the price list and get the money. He showed up with a two thousand dollar price tag. He was disappointed but got over it. In a short time, things calmed down. It's all part of the learning process. Stewart learned quickly and continues to play an important role in all we do in Mazatlán.

Property and Bureaucracy

One of the dumbest things that you can do is help build a church clinic, feeding center, or any structure without knowing who the legal owner of the land is. You don't know how many stories I have heard of dumb gringos or rookie missionaries helping to build, only to find out later that it was private property. The way that church property in other countries is registered and deeded is never as simple and easy as it is in the United States. In Mexico, church property can be very complicated. In 1859, President Benito Juarez nationalized all church property. All churches became federal property. The reason he did this was to break the power of the Catholic Church. During that time, the church had become very powerful and wealthy. Juarez was leading the fight against the French for independence, and the Catholic Church was backing the French. He responded by making all church properties government properties.

When I began my work in Mexico, that's the system that I encountered. It was a shock to my culturally formed American thinking. Not only the land and the building were government property, but the furnishings also. There were a lot of challenges we had to deal with. At that time, the Mexican government was highly centralized, so everything was done in Mexico City. Permission was required from religious affairs in Mexico City before making any changes to the church building. If you wanted to add on a Sunday school room or a bathroom, you needed permission before you could start construction. As you know, any time you deal with government bureaucracy, things happen slowly. Add to the mix the anti-Protestant feelings that were present at the time, and you get a picture of the obstacles we had to deal with.

One missionary made the fatal mistake of registering the land with the government where he wanted to build a church, and then sometime later he requested permission from religious affairs to build a church. He was denied. These factors compelled us to do things in a certain way. We knew that we couldn't buy land in the name of the church and then expect to build afterward with any certainty of a reasonable time frame.

During that time, most Protestants would put the property in the name or names of individuals. Sometimes it would take them years to finish the church. Afterward they would register it with the government. Doing things that way presented some dangers, but the difficulty of dealing with religious affairs and the cost of making trips to the religious affairs office in Mexico City made it the only viable option.

If you plan on helping to build a church (or any building), never assume the church is the legal owner of the land that you are going to build on. To avoid being the dumb gringo and throwing money away, you will need to ask some pointed questions. Here are a few tips on what to ask:

1. Does the land have a deed? If so, whose name is it in? Ask for a photocopy for your records. If they plan on building first and then registering it to avoid all the

hassles with religious affairs, it's best to have the names of the people on the deed.

2. Sometimes in Mexico it takes years for land to be cleared for the official deed. If that's the case, be sure to get copies of the papers that they have.

3. Do the church members know whose name the deed is in? If not, it should be announced publicly before you assist with any construction.

4. If the land deed is not in the name of the church, explain that you can only help if the legal owners draft a letter stating that the land is for the church and will not be sold. If possible, do a notarized letter.

5. Post a copy of the letter in the church, and make sure the leaders have a copy.

6. Ask for receipts for building materials that are purchased for the church construction. Leave some preaddressed stamped envelopes to facilitate things.

7. Continue to monitor the progress. Check back with them to see when the land will be registered as a church.

Follow these instructions to avoid falling into the big dumb category. It doesn't matter how long you have known the native pastor that you are helping, nor does it matter how much you trust him or her. Who cares if you lose your warm fuzzy feeling because you are afraid the native pastor thinks you do not trust him?

You might want to develop a standard list of requirements necessary to receive any financial assistance. To not provide accountability for national pastors who have been raised in a culture of corruption is a grave disservice to them. Sometimes we don't do it because we don't want to feel colonial or untrusting. In order to stroke our own ego, we place them in an unhealthy position with money.

Always remember, missions is not about you or how you feel. This is something I have had to learn many times over. This point came to my attention recently when a Mexican official was the guest speaker of a nonreligious group made up of Canadians and Americans who hold a monthly breakfast. Each month they invite a different speaker and then take a collection for their charity of the month. The speaker that month shared how he had given a ten thousand peso ($1,000 USD) grant to a local school. Then he stated, "You don't think I just handed them the money, do you?" I could almost read his mind. He was thinking, "You dumb gringos better learn from what I'm telling you." He then went on to share how he administered the money. He asked the school administrators what the first thing was that they wanted to do. "Paint some of the classrooms," they replied. He then purchased the paint and delivered it to the school. When they finished painting, he asked them what else they needed and purchased those items as well.

A missionary or mission worker that suffers colonial missionary complex will have trouble operating in this fashion. He or she will fear that he's too controlling or dominating. This missionary will feel more comfortable handing the money over with no or very little accountability required. This is what I call modern mission colonialism. I believe the root problem of colonial missions was the lack or absence of respect for the culture, including all amoral and positive aspects of the native cultures. The missionaries would ignore the culture and do things the way they deemed necessary. If missions people ignore how the local churches ensure accountability and do it the way they deem necessary, then that's modern colonialism though it's cloaked in the pretense of showing the natives that you trust them. Even though you would never consciously say this, you are stating, "I reject what your culture says because my judgment is superior to yours. I will do it my way."

Some Helpful Tips

If you are working with a working-class pastor, there are several ways to help him or her without the church getting the perception that you will meet all of his or her needs. Take a look at the pastor's Bible. Could the pastor use a better one? Consider getting him or her a good study Bible with a good concordance. Let me reiterate: Don't give him or her the money to buy one; you buy it and give it to the pastor. Find out what study materials the church has. Does the pastor need some of the basics, such as a Bible dictionary? Perhaps the pastor could use a book on sermon preparation. Try to find out his or her needs. However, you don't want to give him or her a stack of books at one time. Find out the ages of the pastor's children and bring in an extra suitcase of used clothes. If you bring used clothes for the pastor and his or her family, any clothes that they use is money they don't have to spend on new clothes. You have contributed to them economically at virtually no cost to yourself, and you gave no appearance that you have money to throw around. If the pastor has a car, take a look at the tires. If they are on their last treads, that would be a way to help out. But you need to do it without drawing unneeded attention to yourself. Once again, don't hand over money. Go to the tire place with him or her and pay for the tires.

Churches can always use any type of sound equipment—microphones and the like. You might want to check with your sound people at your church. They might have several things sitting in storage that are no longer used. Dust it off and take it to the mission field. In Latin America, the guitar is still the instrument of choice. New worship leaders are in need of guitars. You might want to put an announcement in your church bulletin asking anyone who has a guitar in their closet to donate it. When I go to the United States on vacation, I always buy a cheap guitar to play as we are traveling. These days, you can get a pretty good-playing guitar for around a hundred bucks. When I return to Mexico, I look for a developing worship leader to give the guitar to. Most of the time, instead of giving the person the guitar, I will loan it. That way, if the person does not continue, I can ask for the guitar back. If the person proves faithful, you can give them the guitar.

Some time back, one of our missionaries contacted the leader of our missions partnership in the United States. He was going to team up with a Mexican national to plant a church and wanted the partnership to buy them a PA system. The U.S. leader contacted me and wanted to know what I thought we should do. Neither one of us knew if the plant would survive. However, I wanted to give them a chance without risking the loss of the investment in a new PA. We agreed to loan them a PA. If the plant made it, we could always give them the system at a later date. In this case, the church didn't make it. The PA was passed on to another new plant. If we had given them the PA up-front, we wouldn't have had a voice as to where it went when the church shut down. By helping in these ways, you can give needed financial assistance without creating a dependency or the perception that the church doesn't need to support the pastor because he or she now has a sugar daddy.

CHAPTER 7

The Mazatlán Four-Point Strategy

Many factors will have to go into the equation to develop a workable strategy: the culture, economics, city versus village, big city (a million-plus inhabitants) versus smaller cities (one hundred thousand or more), small rural towns, receptivity/hostility toward the Gospel, and effectiveness of highly visible events versus low-key evangelism. Let me state once again, strategies and methods are *not* the most important part of your work. Living with the people, true humility, loving the people, and respecting their culture is the starting point.

Having said that, I believe that the Mazatlán Four-Point Strategy will be effective in most Latin American countries. The Mazatlán strategy emerged from our work in central Mexico in Fresnillo, Zacatecas. When we started, we really didn't have a clear strategy. Our goal was to win souls and start churches. In those days, Zacatecas was one of the most difficult areas of Mexico in which to work. Less than 0.1 percent of the population was evangelicals. When my wife and I arrived there in the late seventies, there was only one church in the whole state that had reached one hundred in attendance. Success was measured first by surviving as a plant, and then by having a solid group of twenty-five or thirty adults. Breaking the fifty-person attendance barrier was considered very successful. Just starting a church that survived was a major victory. In the early years, the idea of having a church of two hundred was like a megachurch. It had never been done.

I started out in Fresnillo (population 150,000) and planted the first church. I did two things that were radical and new for that area of Mexico. I rented a local theater for an evangelistic crusade and put together a band (somewhat rock-and-rollish) for the event. People in that area had been so indoctrinated against Protestants that they feared going into a Protestant church. Being in a theater brought down that barrier. During those days, there were very few secular bands and no Christian groups. So, having a decent Christian rock band was an attraction. The event was a success by Zacatecas standards, and a church was born that survived. I eventually left that church with another missionary who was working with me and began to plant churches in some of the smaller towns (with populations of twenty thousand to fifty thousand) within a fifty-mile radius of Fresnillo.

After planting four churches in small towns, I felt that it was time to plant another in Fresnillo. There was a big building for rent downtown on the main road. It used to be a farm tractor dealership. The area where they displayed the tractors had a roof with two open sides. It was perfect for public events and for showing Christian movies. There was also plenty of office space and a closed-in warehouse that would be perfect for church services. The only problem was that I didn't have any money. We were still shoestring budget missionaries.

During the time that I was planting the small-town churches, I continued to live in Fresnillo. One day I went to pay my rent and ask my landlord if he knew who owned the big building for rent downtown. "I do," he replied. "Are you interested in renting?" I told him I didn't know but that I would like to look at it. He handed me a ring of keys and told me to go check it out. I went and looked it over and thought, "This is perfect for what we want to do." Later on, I returned the keys, and he asked me what I thought of the building. "Well, I like the building, and I think it would be perfect for us," I told him. "Would you like to rent it?" he asked again. "I'm going to be honest with you," I replied. "I don't have the money to rent it. I'm broke. I don't even have fifty dollars in my checking account. I would love to have that building to start a church in, but I can't."

What happened next totally caught me by surprise. "Here's what we can do," he explained. "I'll draw up a contract for three years for X amount." I don't remember the amount after all these years, but it was reasonable. He then went on and explained that he would forfeit the customary deposit, and since I didn't have any money at the time, the rent would be paid at the end of the month instead of the first of the month. The next day, I signed a three-year lease, not knowing how I was going to pay for it, but I sensed the hand of the Lord on it. Thirty days later, I struggled to scrape together the first rent payment. I was broke again and wondered if I had made a mistake signing a three-year lease.

A short time later, something happened that was completely unexpected and would change everything: The Mexican peso underwent a massive devaluation. The dollar shot up, and the peso fell. The dollar gained so much that after converting dollars into pesos to pay the rent, it was only $150 USD. I couldn't believe it. For $150 a month, I had a big building (around twenty thousand square feet, if I remember correctly) on the main street through downtown, and it was locked in for three years.

The groundwork was in place to start a new church. Being a downtown church made it appealing to more than just poor folks. We began to penetrate the middle and professional class. Schoolteachers, doctors, and business people were now attending. At first we didn't see the need for having multiple churches in the same town. We did a lot of outreaches and ministry around town in the poor colonias, but we expected them to come to the central church.

When the three-year lease was up, we bought land. Most of our energy was now focused on building our own church building. During that time, I continued to minister to the poor colonias in Fresnillo. One strategy I was experimenting with was identifying a need that no one was meeting, and then trying to meet it as a way that opened the door for the Gospel. In Fresnillo, one of the biggest problems was water shortages.

Quenching a Colonia's Thirst

A combination of factors were behind the problem. The water mains were always breaking. The word on the street was that the man in charge of putting in the mains installed a pipe that didn't meet specifications and pocketed the rest of the money. It may well have been the case with corruption so prevalent at that time. Another factor was that the populace needed more wells but did not have the money to drill them. That once again goes back to the corruption factor. Mismanagement was also a big part of the problem. When builders initially hooked up the water lines to the homes, they didn't have any meters, so it was run into the house. Then the shut-off valve was installed. There was no way to shut off the water from outside without digging up the street and cutting the pipe. That was a recipe for disaster. Most people simply didn't pay their water bill. There was little that the city could do to make them pay. It would have been too much work and too expensive to dig up all the lines, cut them, and then put in shut-off valves. No one feared having their water cut off.

However, with the light company, the situation was the extreme opposite. The day after your light bill was due, if gone unpaid, you were cut off. It was amazing how people always managed to pay their light bills on time. When they knew that punishment was imminent, they complied. What a sermon illustration. When people don't fear immediate punishment, their conduct reflects it.

Eventually the townsfolk would have to pay the piper. The day came when the chickens came home to roost. The water company didn't have the money to pay its light bill. The light company acted accordingly and shut off the water company's lights. There was no electricity to run the wells or pumps. A city of 150,000 people was entirely out of water. It went on for three days as the water company blamed the people for not paying their water bills and the people accused the city of mismanagement. They were both right, but it still made it a lose-lose situation.

This scenario gave me an opportunity to meet a need that no one else was meeting and open doors and hearts for the Gospel. I determined to get a big water tank and take water to the poor. I looked at my options. To have a tank made in Mexico would be expensive. It would have to be made out of steel sheets welded together. It would not only be expensive but very heavy. I would not be able to carry it in my pickup truck. I would have to buy a truck or trailer just for the tank. Back in those days, buying a vehicle in Mexico cost two or three times what it would cost in the United States. It was far beyond my financial possibilities.

I knew that in Texas, farm supply stores sold big plastic tanks made for pickups. They were light enough that one person could move them around. So the main problem facing me was getting the tank past Mexican customs at the border. This was before the North American Free Trade Agreement (NAFTA) between Mexico and the United States was signed. Mexico had a closed border for imports. The only way to get something in was to pay a hefty bribe, and of course, for us, that was out of the question. We didn't want to be part of the problem.

Off I went to the border for another missionary adventure. The dentist who worked in our church clinic in Fresnillo decided to accompany me. We arrived at McAllen, Texas, and did our customary shopping. I purchased a five hundred gallon plastic water tank, which filled up the bed of the truck. I also had a portable cement mixer that someone had given to me, and I decided to take it to Mexico as well.

Let me try to paint a picture of what I was up against. As I said, this was pre-NAFTA. After that treaty was implemented, you could import up to one thousand dollars of new merchandise simply by paying the import tax at the border. There was no limit for computers. The tax was a little stiff at first. It was about 20 to 30 percent, but at least you could do it. Pre-NAFTA required a lot of skill in hiding the articles that you wanted to take in so that the customs inspectors couldn't spot them, or it took good negotiating ability for the amount of bribe if you got caught. Normally, it was best to have items that weren't too big, such as VCRs and TVs.

Now, here I come cruising to the border with a huge water tank and towing a cement mixer. They could see me coming by a country mile. Another thing working against me was that I couldn't pass myself off as a tourist going to Mexico. At that time, missionaries had to sneak in as tourists. The customs officials could be quite unfriendly if they discovered that you were a missionary. They were all staring at me as I pulled up and parked. The next step was to go inside and get a visa and permit to take the vehicle into Mexico. I went into stealth mode and did my best goofy tourist imitation. I only spoke English to those who issue the visas. To speak Spanish would have blown my cover and put me in danger of being refused a visa or have caused them to reduce the amount of time that I could stay in Mexico from the customary six months to thirty days or less.

Things went smoothly getting the papers, but now the real battle was about to begin: getting inspected and cleared to go. The ol' "I'm just a tourist" trick was not an option. Tourists don't drive around with five hundred gallon water tanks in the back of their trucks, towing cement mixers. The first round started out as I expected, with the customs inspector shaking his head and saying, "You can't bring those things into Mexico." I sparred back explaining how I was going to use the tank to serve the poor. Back and forth we went as he waited for me to offer a bribe, which I wasn't going to do. He walked off to let us think about it and inspected another car. He returned a little while later, still waiting for me to make an offer. He soon became impatient with no forthcoming offer and went into his air-conditioned glass office.

My veteran discernment was telling me that we were making progress. I had been through many border-crossing battles, most of which I won, and I could usually sense when we were heading to victory. I waited for a little while longer before going into his office to continue. To go in too soon would have appeared too pushy. Timing is also important. You don't want to go in when the official is dealing with someone else, either. I waited until things weren't busy in his small office and made my approach. I continued to plead my case and began to sense that victory was close. Suddenly, slightly raising his voice, he said, "OK, you give me any amount of money you want, and you can go. I don't care if you just give me one dollar. Give me whatever you want and go." He caught me totally off-guard. Should I give him one dollar and get out of there before he changed his mind?

I asked him to wait while I went to consult with my companion Juan. "Juan, he says that if I only give him one dollar that we can go. What do you think?" Juan reminded me that I had stated that we wouldn't pay any bribes. I slowly made my way back to the office, expecting the worst. From his point of view, he was being more than generous. "I'm sorry, I can't pay any amount," I said as I explained once again that we weren't going to make any money doing this. His body language and facial expression told me that he was upset. "OK, go ahead," he told me, the tone of his voice communicating his frustration. As I was on my way out the door, he stopped me and said, "If you have any trouble at the thirty [that's the next customs check thirty kilometers down the road], tell Commander So-and-So that I said it's OK." The rest of the trip went smoothly on our return to Fresnillo.

I was now ready to continue with my new experiment. I went to a private well, paid a few dollars to fill the tank, and set out to deliver the water. As I was giving out water in a poor colonia, someone told me about a new colonia that didn't have any water, meaning that they didn't have any water lines and as a result never even got occasional water pressure.

In Mexico, whenever a new colonia is started, it's done in the opposite way that we do it. In the United States, when a subdivision is developed, before any building starts, the sewer and water lines are put in, the electrical lines are installed, the streets are paved, and phone and cable TV lines are put in. Well, in Mexico, with poor colonias, it's completely different. The lots and the streets are marked off, and people start building their shacks. They have no services. They have no water, no electricity, and of course cable TV and phones are not even considered.

It was pretty easy to identify this need that no one was meeting. The folks in the new colonia didn't have any clean drinking water at all. I searched and found this newly developing colonia on the edge of town. To get clean water, the people there had to go to a neighboring colonia at three in the morning with their buckets. In many cities of Mexico, you only have water pressure certain hours of the day. Everyone has water storage tanks so that whenever there is water pressure, you can fill the tank. The public faucet happened to have water pressure at 3 a.m. What a burden to get up at 3 a.m. and take two five-gallon buckets to haul water back to your humble home. In the high mountains of Zacatecas, it can get very cold and windy as well.

Two days a week I made the rounds and gave each family ten

gallons of water. We were becoming quite popular in the colonia. One day, as I was delivering water, I had an experience that would set the pattern for a lot of our future works. I am not sure what terminology to use—God showed me, God spoke to me, or God impressed upon me. In a few seconds, God showed me that he wanted me to get land in the colonia and build a children's feeding and ministry center. The feeding center would eventually become a church.

Leftists Doing the Right Thing

It was also impressed upon me the importance of getting into new colonias as soon as possible. What I didn't know at the time was that the colonia where I was to get the land was controlled by the communist party, and they weren't thrilled with my new revelation. At one point, the party leaders informed me that they would never give me land in their colonia and told me not to ask again. A year-and–a-half battle would ensue, with prayer being my only weapon. At times, I questioned whether God had showed me anything. I was tempted to think that I invented it all. God never spoke to me. But despite the doubt, I persevered in prayer. It took over a year, but eventually the communist leaders sought me out to let me know that they had changed their minds and had land for me.

Sometimes, when we are in the middle of a battle, we cannot see everything God wants to accomplish. When it looked like we would never be given land in the communist-controlled colonia, I began to check on available lots in the neighboring colonia, but it was like Paul in Acts 16:7 trying to go to Bithynia and the Holy Spirit wouldn't let him. After the battle was won, I could see God's strategy. There was only one political group left where we didn't have favor. We had earned the respect and favor of every other political group, even the one that was considered anti-Protestant. Now God wanted to bring the communists into the fold.

Other things were happening during the year and a half as we battled in prayer for the promised land. We had some friends and admirers even among the leftists. As word got around that they wouldn't give me land, some of the party members began to speak up for us. One of the leaders told me after the fact that rank-and-file members were asking the leader why he wouldn't give Brother Fred (that's how I was known even outside the church) land in the colonia. God was working all the time, but we would not know that until the battle was over.

Here's how it finally played out. After a year and a half of prayer, discouragement, doubt, and pressing on, one of the colonia leaders came to my house, looking for me. I wasn't home at the time, but he informed my wife that they were going to give me a lot. He wanted me to contact him immediately. When I arrived home and heard the news, I was ecstatic. It seemed unreal. I immediately set out for the colonia. On the way there, I began to regain my confidence. It was God who spoke to me about getting into the colonia! I didn't imagine it! God was with me, and the communists had resisted God! I would now raise the price of poker. They would have to pay for messing with God.

When I arrived at the colonia, two of the leaders were waiting for me. They had a large map of the neighborhood with the available lots marked. "Which would you like?" one of them asked me. I replied, "I don't want one lot; I want two." "Nobody has two lots," the party president protested. "Well, I need two lots," I shot back with a voice of confidence. "OK," he replied. "Let me see if we have two lots together." We ended up with twice the land that we had originally asked for. The short version is that we acquired four lots. I was finally beginning to understand what God was up to. We were soon busy building our first colonia project.

I believe that one of the fears of the communist leader was losing the affection of the poor. I was known as a friend of the poor and downtrodden. I think he was concerned that I would move into his colonia and take his place in the hearts of the people.

After we finished our building, we planned a new shoe give-away for the children of the colonia. We traced the footprints of the children on a sheet of paper and distributed the sheets to our U.S. churches. They in turn would look for individuals to sponsor a child. We then took the packages of shoes into Mexico to hand them out to the sponsored children at Christmas. Taking into consideration the fears of some of the leftist leaders, I had them coordinate the tracing of the children's feet. I gave the leader the microphone and stayed in the background. We did the same thing at

Christmas when the shoes were distributed. Their attitude toward me became very positive. After a while, they wanted me up-front with them. Then they began to publicly recognize and thank me whenever we had any outreaches to the poor.

Later, in a general meeting of the whole colonia, they presented me with an award for service to the colonia and the poor. It was signed by all the leftist leaders. I still have it displayed in my house as a reminder of how God works. The complete battle had been won. The land was just part of it. The leftists were now our newest best buddies. In the ensuing elections they won three mayorships in the state for the first time and invited me to accompany them to take power.

The Strategy Defined

Here's the simple four-point Mazatlán strategy that began to emerge in central Mexico and was refined in Mazatlán. It gives four main components in a simple form and leaves flexibility to adapt them to the situation.

1. Start the first church where you can reach the middle and professional class people. This will become the mother church, or central church.
2. As soon as possible after the central church is established, begin to plant branch churches.
3. Make the branch churches community centers.
4. Get land ASAP in any new colonias that are being developed. *Colonia* is the word used in Mexico for *suburb* or *addition*. Mexican cities are divided into districts called *colonias*. Usually each colonia has a political leader for any dealings with city hall.

Here's the thinking behind the Mazatlán strategy.

Start the first church where middle-class and professional people can be reached.
Our goal in missions is always to establish churches that become self-supporting and self-governing. By starting with middle- and

professional-class people, you can reach that goal sooner. Unlike in the United States, the middle class in Mexico is much smaller, so you need to target them. We don't target professionals because they are better than the poor. Nor do we respect churches that only want middle- and upper-class congregations. We are, after all, social economic classes. By starting with professionals, it helps us to reach this goal of reaching as many people as possible from all social classes.

Another reason for starting with the professional and middle class is that it's easier to raise up pastors and leaders. In Mexico, the general rule is that you can only minister or lead at your own social level or those below your social level. Of course, there are exceptions to the cultural rule. In Fresnillo, when I turned the work over to a national and moved to Mazatlán, the church had about 30 percent professionals. The new man was not middle or professional class. Now, several years later, the church is 50 percent professional. However, that is not always the case.

There is a clear reason why the professional class can provide leadership for the church For example, by having schoolteachers, you not only have people who can learn quickly but people who can often minister above their social economic class. A teacher is also highly respected by the lower classes. I am by no means advocating that leadership should be made up only of professional-class people. In the overall leadership team, as many different social classes as possible should be represented. But getting started is best if you can start with the middle class and up.

Another reason to start the first church where professionals are reached for Christ is that it will provide a pool of people who can help when you start ministering to the poor. If you start with the poor, then where will you get the doctors and dentists that you will need to be able to minister to them? You will narrow down your options, and you will have to hire a doctor or dentist in order to do that type of ministry.

By starting our first church in Mazatlán in what they call the Golden Zone, we were able to reach into the professional class. Soon, we had three dentists attending our services. Two of them volunteer in our clinics, and the other dentist volunteers when we do field clinics. We are able to operate two dental clinics because of their willingness to serve the poor of Mazatlán. We recently sent one of our dentists to Nicaragua to assist a group of Americans on a mission trip there.

I am not saying that starting a church with the professional class is the only way to do it. However, I think it's the best option whenever you can do it that way. But, if you have to hire a doctor or dentist, God bless you. I understand that everyone can't plant a professional-class church. At times, the area of the country where you work is rural or poor.

We did have an unexpected benefit as a result of having our clinics staffed by native dentists. Other local medical people became aware of our work and wanted to volunteer as well. One day a lady contacted me who represented a group of medical personnel desiring to serve the poor. They had observed how we work, liked our professionalism and organization, and desired to work with us. That probably would not have happened if we had been paying our dentist.

If you start some children's feeding centers, you will need capable people to run them. To purchase food to feed one to three hundred will require someone with a car and ability to calculate the quantities of food to be purchased. This person will probably come from the central church.

If you start reaching only the poor, it's slower and harder to raise up the needed pastors, leaders, and infrastructure. Remember, the first church will become the central church that assists the branch churches. The central church will provide office support. In Mexico, a church in a poor colonia cannot afford things like copy machines and computers. That's where the central church comes in. The colonia churches will have access to copiers to help them with their Sunday school and other programs. They will also need help making overheads for their worship services. Those are just some of the advantages. In Mazatlán, some of the colonia churches have the office keep the offerings. Having a central church office helps the colonia churches feel more connected and part of something bigger than their own little church.

As soon as the central church is established, begin to plant branch churches.

There are numerous reasons why five churches of two hundred people are better than one church of one thousand people. Christian Swartz, whom I mentioned earlier, did an extensive study of churches around the world. His research revealed that a church of one hundred to two hundred people had a higher percentage of growth than a megachurch. In other words, five churches of two hundred will grow at a much faster rate than one church of one thousand people. It's also much more difficult to find someone with the ability and gifting to pastor a church of one thousand or more.

In Mexico, it's very easy to reach children, but you need to have a presence in their neighborhoods in order to do so. By having a church out in the local neighborhoods (colonias), you can have an effective children's ministry. These children would never be able to come to the central church. In Mazatlán, we have around one thousand attending Saturday Bible clubs in several of our branch churches. These numbers are not included in the church attendance figures. So, in Mexico, the impact of five small churches versus one big church results in many more people being reached who don't show up on the statistic sheets.

Another logical reason to plant branch churches is so that more people are involved in ministry. For example, a church of one thousand might have two worship bands, whereas five churches of two hundred will have between five to ten worship bands. In a big church, the bar is always higher for musicians, preachers, and other ministers. Less professionalism is required and expected in a smaller church. I am in no way saying that no one should have a big church. But the truth is, those with the ability to plant a church that will grow to five thousand are few and far between. If you can plant a megachurch, then by all means, do it. But if you don't have the vision to spin off new church plants, you will minimize your effectiveness and potential.

There are several ways to go about planting branch churches. One way is to build a children's feeding center first. In Mexico, 48 percent of children are undernourished, according to government studies. That presents us with a perfect opportunity to make a difference and show the love of Christ in a practical way. By starting with a feeding center, the building will be seen not as a church but as a building where children are fed. When it is time to plant a church, the community should have a positive view of you and the building. The best approach won't be to announce, "We're starting a church," but to say, "We're starting services in the feeding center." Remember, when you use the word *church*, your concept of the word may differ radically from that of the people in the community.

I relearned this lesson again as we prepared to have a public dedication of a new feeding center. A Mexican businessman spent around forty thousand dollars building a children's feeding center for us in a poor colonia. He was our guest of honor for the inauguration. However, he invited some political friends who were campaigning for office. I expressed some concern since our name was on the building. Mexico is very strict about the separation of church and state. When I mentioned my concerns to him, he said, "Don't worry—you're a Christian community, not a church." My impulse was to burst out in a theological tantrum proclaiming us to be the church. However, as I thought about it, I realized he was right. By his definition of church, we weren't one. To him the word *church* meant an institution, not a community of believers. It wasn't the right time to bring up theology. My point is, do not insist on using terms that mean one thing to you and something else to those to whom you minister.

By no means limit your church planting to starting a feeding center first. It's just one way to do it. However, at times it will be the only way. In 2000, we heard about a newly forming colonia in a town near Mazatlán. We inquired about getting land for the church. The committee that controlled land distribution didn't want a church there, at least not a Protestant one. When we shared our plans to have a children's feeding center, they changed their position and gave us land. Because of the lack of funds, we weren't able to build the feeding center right away and decided to start the church first. The nationals put in four wood poles, built a tar paper roof, and started services. After about a year with no feeding center, the committee let us know that they were considering taking the land back. In Mexico, when a new colonia is developed, it can take years before the land title is issued by the federal government. Since we had no permanent structure on the land, we were vulnerable to having it taken and given to someone else. The tar paper roof wasn't enough since no one was living there. I call this practice the "shopping cart law." When you go to a store and grab a shopping cart, your right to the cart is contingent on you having something in the cart. If you turn your back on the cart and you have nothing in it, then someone can grab it and be on their way. It's too late. You can't go around the store looking for your cart. So in some cases, starting a feeding center will be the only way to get into certain colonias. But never limit the power of the Gospel to your ability to give something away to be successful.

Some time back, I was at a conference that was hosted by a large church in the Los Angeles area. One of the pastors in charge of the missions and benevolence ministries wanted to talk with me. During the course of our conversation, he shared about a Saturday night service that his church had for Hispanics that had an attendance of five hundred. After a few questions, the secret of his success was revealed. Everyone who attended got a bag of groceries. Man, woman, child, or baby, if you were breathing, you got a bag of food after the service was over. "You don't have a church—you have a crowd," I told him. "If you want to find out, give the food away on Friday and announce that no groceries will be given out at the church service." Very good advice, but as I look back, I realize I was probably too blunt and direct. I gave him too much truth all at once, and I most likely made him feel like a dumb gringo. They never sought me out for another opinion. I do not know if they took my advice. Even though technically I was right, in my zeal I came on too strong.

Having said that, let me state emphatically that you should never require someone to attend a religious service in order to receive something. It sends the wrong message to those in need and gives a false image of how many people are really interested in the gospel. As I already mentioned, giving away food and clothes has become a hindrance to the Gospel in some border towns. On occasions, I have had American pastors share with me about growing Hispanic communities in their towns and their desire to minister to them. Their plan is always to give away food and clothes. I tell them that when you share the Gospel with a Mexican, you don't have to hand him or her a bag of clothes or food first. It seems ingrained into their thinking that to reach Mexicans, you have to give them something. I always encourage them to not lock themselves into that mindset. Mexicans are much better than Americans at discerning who is humble and who's not. Go to them with a humble heart and love for the people, and they'll receive you with or without a bag of clothes to give away.

Another way to plant branch churches is to send teams from the central church to evangelize a colonia. We have done this in Mazatlán. After making a few converts, we send our bus and start a bus route to bring people in to the central church for services. Whenever you reach the desired number, you can break them off and start a branch church. To ensure the success of the new plant, we suspend the bus pick up to the central church. The number of people needed in Mexico to start a branch church is low. The typical colonia church is only twenty to fifty adults, plus kids. The threshold number will vary from country to country. In Mexico, with twenty adults you are off to a good start.

Look for new ways to accelerate church planting. However, you should never look for new ways to do things just so you'll be doing something new. Be careful of the arrogant "I'm cutting-edge" attitude. We do things to be effective and fruitful, not to be cutting-edge. From my experience, new methods are usually rooted in something in the past, whether it be a personal experience or something you have learned from someone else.

Sometime in the future, we are going to try a church plant using an experimental method. We want to put together a team that will include different gifts such as a pastor, evangelist, children's teachers, people who do mercy ministry, and so forth. We want to send them to a colonia where we have already acquired land and have them set up shop for a month or more. They will live in tents or campers and have nightly services. This is not some wild thing I have dreamed up just to say I am doing something that no one else is doing. This has emerged from our experiences with tent crusades over the years. We began to notice that the longer the crusade, the more fruit would remain. Very often the short-term events of two or three days left no permanent fruit. Based on that experiment and other factors, some day we'll do the thirty-day experiment.

Become a Community Center

In many Latin American countries, people have been taught to never enter a Protestant church. Because of this, many people are uncomfortable and even afraid to enter an Evangelical church. If we make our facilities into a place that ministers to people's needs, then that perception can change. Of course, if you have already started a feeding center before the church plant, then you are on your way and need to build around that foundation.

Here are some of the things that we have done in Mazatlán. We joined together with a local beautician's college. They were looking for places for their students to practice, and we had the infrastructure with our feeding centers in poor colonias. We provided a roof, bathrooms, and electricity, and they provided free beauty care for women and haircuts for all. We also worked with a group that taught poor women how to sew and make clothes. They provided the teachers and all the necessary equipment, and the course was held at one of our church/feeding centers. We have also worked with non-Christian doctors. We even allowed a drama group that focused on reaching youth to run a program in one of our places. In one developing colonia, the local school consisted of a few tar paper classrooms. One of our feeding centers was very close to the school and was the biggest building in the neighborhood. So when they wanted to have a special event, they came to us, and we let them use our building.

When you do practical things for people, their response will be that they like having you around. Late one night, a lady saw a drug user breaking into one of our feeding centers. As he would haul stuff out to his hiding place and return for more items, the neighbor lady carried to her own house what he had dropped off. He made several trips without noticing that his stash was gone. Eventually the police arrived and arrested him. All of our kitchenware was safe in the neighbor's house.

Be creative and invent some new ways to be a community

center. It's just a matter of being open to all of the possibilities.

Buy land in new colonias.
In Mexico, Protestants have always been at a disadvantage with the government. For many years, whenever a new colonia was developed, the Catholic Church was automatically given land. It was almost always a large lot in the center of the colonia. Protestants had to buy land, and if they knew you wanted it for a church, the authorities often refused any land.

Another hindrance is the poverty factor. In Mexico, most of the churches are poor working-class. That has changed since I first arrived in the early 1980s. But still, the majority are poor working-class churches. They are always struggling just to survive. Having no favor with the government made it virtually impossible for them to get land in new developments.

Let me inject that things have changed a lot in Mexico over the years. With postmodern thinking influencing Mexico, the government will on occasion donate land to Protestants. Their openness varies from region to region.

The main reason why you want to get into new colonias is because people are more receptive to the Gospel. It's important to begin working the sooner the better. It's good to start as soon as a few people begin to build their houses. By starting early in the development of the colonia, you will become a part of the community.

This strategy will require vision and patience. There may only be twenty families when you begin. You may feel funny building a children's feeding center with so few people living in the colonia, but that's exactly what you want to do. If you are an accepted part of the colonia, it will positively affect how new families moving into the area relate to you. You are not the outsider trying to get into their long established colonia, but the group who was there before they arrived. *They* are the newcomers. That can totally change the way they see you.

A social dynamic comes into play when you are able to start a work in a new development. The new arrivals have already disrupted their social networks. Friendships and relationships from years back are affected. When they move into the new colonia, they will begin to form new social networks. If you are there before they arrive, your chances of becoming part of their new circle of friends increases.

To Sum It Up

Many things are important concerns in missions. Methods and strategy have their place. Becoming as fluent as possible in learning the language is wise. Understanding the culture of those to whom you are called to minister is important. Having knowledge of the history of missions can be helpful. Several factors can be good, important, and useful, but all will be in vain without true passion.

Passion will make up for deficiencies in other areas. I've witnessed it several times when nationals have embraced missionaries whose skill in Spanish was lacking. Some spoke very poor Spanish, but you would never know it by the way the Mexicans accepted them. They weren't great theologians or experts in missionary strategy or history. But they had passion and a heart for the people. Mexicans could sense that and responded by receiving them and showing them great respect. These missionaries then became successful, which should be the goal of missions.

I believe that modern missions will be hindered by men and women who have studied missions and have been trained to be overly concerned about the mistakes of the colonial missionaries. This approach, in turn, will cause them to develop a mechanical way in which they relate to nationals, always worrying about being "over" them or not installing them as leaders soon enough.

However, I believe that the greatest damage may be done by those whose goal is to do missions in a "new" way. Determining to do missions in a new way is one of the stupidest things you can do. Mission societies, ministries, missions task forces, and mission boards that try to do this are setting themselves up for disaster. However, they won't realize it until years down the road when the fruit of their endeavors is ripe. Many things that colonial missions did were new at the time, and the damage they caused wasn't realized until many years later.

I've done many things on the mission field that were new, but my expressed goal was never to do something new or different. My goal was to be fruitful or successful, not to do missions in a new way. In our quest for success in reaching the lost, we would sometimes come up with methods and strategies that were completely new. The goal should be "How can I be successful?" not "How can I do missions in a new way that no one else has done?" That attitude has a smack of arrogance to it. If your goal is not to do missions like the colonial missionaries, you probably won't be very successful.

Build upon the successes of others. When new methods and strategies are rooted in successful missions from the past, or when new ways are born out of years of observation on the field, then the probability of fruitfulness is greater. I've grown tired of people who've never lived on the mission field coming up with new strategies.

Summing it up in one paragraph, be passionate and love people. Build upon past successes, on that which has worked. Draw upon history and personal experience to develop methods and strategies, making being successful your goal. If you happen to do things that are new or different, so be it. And, remember that money can either help or hinder missions work. Make sure that you know the difference. May your money and other resources be used in such a way that God is glorified.

May God bless you in your missions endeavors!

Printed in the United States
45924LVS00001BA/205-519

9 781594 677120